10.31.06

For Earl,

whose work I admire
& whose article on Jorge de
Lima I still nurture hopes
of acquiring!
I hope this collection may
be of interest to you, for
its many connections with
your own fields of inquiry.

abraços,
alexandra

NEW DIRECTIONS IN LATINO AMERICAN CULTURES

A series edited by Licia Fiol-Matta and José Quiroga

**Published in 2004:**

*New Tendencies in Mexican Art,*
by Rubén Gallo

*Jose Martí: An Introduction,*
by Oscar Montero

**Published in 2003:**

*Bilingual Games: Some Literary Investigations,*
edited by Doris Sommer

*Tongue Ties: Logo-Eroticism in Anglo-Hispanic Literature,*
by Gustavo Perez-Firmat

*Velvet Barrios: Popular Culture & Chicana/o Sexualities,*
edited by Alicia Gaspar de Alba, with a foreword by Tomás Ybarra
Frausto

*The Famous 41: Sexuality and Social Control in Mexico, 1901,*
edited by Robert McKee Irwin, Edward J. McCaughan, and Michele
Rocío Nasser

*New York Ricans from the Hip Hop Zone,*
by Raquel Rivera

**Forthcoming:**

*None of the Above: Contemporary Puerto Rican Cultures and Politics,*
edited by Frances Negrón-Muntaner

*The Letter of Violence: Essays on Narrative and Theory,*
by Idelber Avelar

# THE MASTERS AND THE SLAVES

## Plantation Relations and *Mestizaje* in American Imaginaries

*Edited by*

*Alexandra Isfahani-Hammond*

THE MASTERS AND THE SLAVES
© Alexandra Isfahani-Hammond, 2005.

First published in 2005 by
PALGRAVE MACMILLAN™
175 Fifth Avenue, New York, N.Y. 10010 and
Houndmills, Basingstoke, Hampshire, England RG21 6XS
Companies and representatives throughout the world.

PALGRAVE MACMILLAN is the global academic imprint of the Palgrave Macmillan division of St. Martin's Press, LLC and of Palgrave Macmillan Ltd. Macmillan® is a registered trademark in the United States, United Kingdom and other countries. Palgrave is a registered trademark in the European Union and other countries.

ISBN 1–4039–6563–3 (hardback)
ISBN 1–4039–6708–3 (paperback)

Library of Congress Cataloging-in-Publication Data

The masters and the slaves : plantation relations and mestizaje in American imaginaries / edited by Alexandra Isfahani-Hammond.
        p.cm.
    Includes bibliographical references and index.
    ISBN 1–4039–6563–3 (cl : alk. paper)—ISBN 1–4039–6708–3 (pbk. : alk. paper)
    1. Miscegenation—America. 2. Hybridity (Social sciences)—Caribbean area. 3. Postcolonialism—Caribbean area. 4. Mestizaje. 5. Racially mixed people—America. 6. Slavery—America. 7. United States—Race relations. I. Isfahani-Hammond, Alexandra.

GN254.M37 2004
306.3'62'097—dc22                                    2004053373

A catalogue record for this book is available from the British Library.

Design by Newgen Imaging Systems (P) Ltd., Chennai, India.

First edition: January 2005

10 9 8 7 6 5 4 3 2 1

Printed in the United States of America.

# Contents

# ACKNOWLEDGMENTS

The idea for this collection evolved in conversations with Susan Meltzer, Leon Honoré, Lydie Moudileno, Moneera al-Ghadeer, and César Braga-Pinto, to whom I am especially grateful for his feedback on my introduction. I am indebted to my students in *Letras* at the Federal University of Pernambuco—Elio Ferreira, Tânia Lima, Sandra Correia, and Lepê—for their insights into Recifean and global race politics. I want to thank the contributors to this volume for their humor and grace in pulling the anthology together, and Licia Fiol-Matta and Gabriella Pearce for their enthusiasm, encouragement, and extraordinary patience. My special thanks go to Azar Isfahani-Hammond for her energy and awareness of "translated experience," Peter Hammond for introducing me to questions of identity politics and authenticity in the first place and Eric Johnson for his presence and for playing devil's advocate. Finally, I am grateful to the Fulbright Foundation and the University of Puerto Rico for funding me, the Federal University of Pernambuco for hosting me, and António Pankino and Alexandre Aranha for housing me as I edited this anthology.

# CONTRIBUTORS

JOSSIANA ARROYO is Associate Professor of Latin American and Caribbean Literatures and Cultures at the University of Michigan, Ann Arbor. Her interests are literatures and cultures of the African diaspora, and the politics of identity, race, gender, and sexuality. She is the author of *Travestismos Culturales: Literatura y Etnografía en Cuba y Brasil* (Editorial Iberoamericana, 2003). Arroyo has also published articles on Brazilian and Caribbean literatures and cultures in *Revista Iberoamericana*, *Revista de Estudios Hispanicos*, and in the anthologies *LusoSex* (University of Minnesota) and *The State of Latino Theater* (Routledge).

CÉSAR BRAGA-PINTO is Assistant Professor of Portuguese and Comparative Literature at Rutgers, the State University of New Jersey. He is the author of *Promessas de História: Assimilação e Discurso Profético no Brasil Colonial* (EDUSP 2004). His research centers on Brazilian cultural studies and colonialism, and on Lusophone African literatures.

RAMÓN GROSFOGUEL is Associate Professor of Ethnic Studies at the University of California, Berkeley and Senior Research Associate of the Maison des Science de l'Homme, in Paris. He has published numerous articles on Caribbean migrations to Western Europe and the United States, and on the political economy of the world-system. Grosfoguel is the author of *Colonial Subjects* (University of California Press, 2003), and coeditor of *The Modern/Colonial/Capitalist World-System in the Twentieth Century* (Greenwood Press, 2002), *Migration, Transnationalization and Race in a Changing New York* (2001), and *Puerto Rican Jam* (1997).

HELENA HOLGERSSON-SHORTER is currently teaching twelfth-grade English at the Hudson School, a private, college-preparatory school in Hoboken, New Jersey. In 2001, she completed her Ph.D. in Comparative Literature at the University of California, Berkeley, concentrating on African American literature and postcolonial literatures of the Caribbean. Her dissertation, *Illegible Bodies and Illegitimate*

*Texts: Paradigms of Mulatta Literature*, reexamines the literary stereotype of the tragic mulatta in the context of the postcolonial subject's interrogation of her subordinate place in the social and racial hierarchy erected by colonialism, and its supporting theories of racial purity and white superiority.

ALEXANDRA ISFAHANI-HAMMOND is Assistant Professor of Literatures of the Americas at the University of Puerto Rico, Rio Piedras. Her interests are literatures of the Greater Caribbean and contemporary Lusophone cultures and literatures. She has published articles in *Lucero*, the *Journal of Afro-Latin American Cultures and Literatures* and *Hispania*. Her book, *Race, Writing and Gilberto Freyre: Critical Readings of Freyre's Essays on Literature and Authorship*, is currently under consideration by EDUSP, UERJ, and EdUFF.

VALERIE KAUSSEN is Assistant Professor of French literature at the University of Missouri-Columbia, where she teaches Francophone Caribbean literature and culture. Her current book project is entitled *Romancing the Peasant: Ethnography and Modernity in the Haitian Roman Paysan*.

LUIZA FRANCO MOREIRA is Associate Professor of Comparative Literature at Binghamton University. Most recently, she edited an anthology of the poetry of Brazilian author Cassiano Ricardo (Global, 2003). She is the author of *Meninos, Poetas & Heróis* (EDUSP, 2001), a study of poetry and ideology in Brazil during the 1930s and 1940s, and *Mulheres de Branco* (EDUSP, 1992), an analysis of the female characters in F. Scott Fitzgerald's *The Great Gatsby*. A translator and poet, Moreira is a regular contributor to the literary journal, *Inimigo Rumor*, in Rio de Janeiro. Her first collection of poetry is entitled *O Exagero do Sol* (Sette Letras, 2001).

NALINI NATARAJAN is Professor of English at the University of Puerto Rico, Rio Piedras and the author of *Handbook of Twentieth-Century Literatures of India* (Westport, 1996) and *Woman and Indian Modernity* (New Orleans, 2002). She has published and teaches in the areas of Caribbean, feminist, and postcolonial theory.

SHREEREKHA SUBRAMANIAN is pursuing her Ph.D. in Comparative Literature at Rutgers, the State University of New Jersey. Her research focuses on imagined communities with the dead resulting from massacres in Haiti and Hindi-speaking India. Her work attempts to decolonize geography while marking an alternate cartographic route from East to West.

# Introduction: Who Were the Masters in the Americas?

*Alexandra Isfahani-Hammond*

"Europe ruled but without governing; governing first was Africa" (*Casa-Grande e Senzala* 5).[1] This quotation is from Gilberto Freyre, the Brazilian sociologist who canonized plantation assimilationism as national leitmotif with the publication of *Casa-Grande e Senzala* in 1933. Because Freyre's celebration of black culture centers on culinary, sexual, and spiritual traditions, it does not disarm normative master/slave, colonizer/colonized oppositions. Instead, African predominance becomes a commonplace without unsettling Europe's historical–material control. The introduction of this quotation in a book dealing with plantation symbolics in the Americas—a book that is launched into a principally U.S. academic market—will be jarring to sensibilities accustomed to paradigms of master/slave relations employed in the United States.

Caribbean narratives of cultural—and, in particular, sexual—intermingling between masters and slaves contrast vividly with the U.S. shame-ridden will to characterize slavery as a historical aberration wiped clean by the northern occupation and "restoration" of democracy to the U.S. south. But while freedom and socioeconomic mobility, rather than racial and cultural assimilation, are the principal myths of U.S. national identity, the spectral weight of plantation sexual violence and miscegenation is demonstrated by the nation's disingenuous shock at the exposure of "known secrets" such as DNA documentation of Thomas Jefferson's relationship with Sally Hemings in 1998. And while it would be unthinkable to deploy African-European contact during slavery as a sign of the nation's "originality," folkloric plantation tropes are constant fixtures in the landscape of U.S. popular culture, from the colonial theme parks of the Old South and the now sanitized image of Aunt Jemima on maple syrup bottles to the reification of black virility in sports arenas and the play of slavery signifiers in contemporary political discourse, wherein southern, plantation-evoking origins are drawn upon as evidence of humility and authenticity.

The sublimation of miscegenation in the U.S. imaginary is redoubled by a geographical displacement. At the same time that the United States denies sexual and cultural "mixing" within the body politic, nostalgia for a preindustrial, plantation past akin to that envisioned by Caribbean elites is key to the national subconscious. Just as the south is characterized as a virtually alien territory prior to abolition and the region's incorporation into the Union, the eroticized plantation is simply situated in an area just south of the nation's borders, in the Caribbean. Indeed, it is a measure of the simultaneous terror and attraction elicited by oppressed and potentially insurrectionary racialized others that the specter of the Haitian Revolution and Cuban socialism coincide with beguiling constructions of the Caribbean as an eroticized relic of slavery, free of the puritan prohibitions and conflicted relations between blacks and whites that mark U.S. culture.

Given the confrontational history of contact between American polities both preceding and following independence—the will to preeminence that motivated colonial expansion and the struggle for geopolitical hegemony subsequent to the formation of nation-states—it should come as no surprise that these discordant conceptualizations of race and nation (Caribbean reifications of *mestizaje* and the U.S. disavowal of slavery and miscegenation) have emerged in dialogue with one another. Since the nineteenth century, Caribbean and Latin American intellectuals forged concepts of national character that undermined U.S. and European indictments of their "degenerative" mixed-race societies. Beginning with José Marti's "nuestra América mestiza" in the 1890s, the plantation *mestizaje*, which until then had been indicted as the source of Cuba's backwardness, was reinterpreted as an emblem of national pride. In the 1930s, Brazil's Gilberto Freyre cast slavery as the origin for assimilation that produced a uniquely inclusive society by contrast with the United States, typified as the epitome of racial violence and hatred.

Whereas Latin America's blurred racial categorization has historically served as a differential marker for constructing the genetic integrity of U.S. whites, this opposition is now complicated by the resonance of contemporary multiculturalism with Latin America's early twentieth-century "mestizo projects." This parallel is certainly not widely acknowledged, except in the academy where *mestizaje*, like hybridization, créolité, and transculturation, has in recent decades gained leverage as a paradigm for cultural evolution typified by reinvention and transformation. Though heralded as a tool for undermining Manichean racial dialectics—and notwithstanding Roberto Fernández Retamar's canonization of Caliban as the emblem for Latin American resistance to U.S. imperialism—in the Caribbean and Latin American polities in which it emerges, *mestizaje* is by no means indicative of democratization. Caribbean state identifications with oppressed blacks have been informed by political projects as disparate as Ché Guevara's entreaty to the Cuban national community to "become black, mulatto, a worker, a peasant,"[2] Gilberto Freyre's totalizing model of the seigniorial incorporation of "black reality" and François "Papa Doc" Duvalier's conceptualization of his *noiriste* dictatorship as the incarnation of the slave's desire for both liberty and containment. In many instances, the reification of the African/slave legacy has been informed by a geopolitical struggle between post-slavery elites, with the United States insisting that it has remained genetically pure, and Latin America's ruling classes proclaiming in an altogether proprietary fashion that they possess something the Yankees do not—that their specimens of African culture are superior and that their ruling bodies, moreover, linguistically and spiritually incorporate them.

*The Masters and the Slaves: Plantation Relations and Mestizaje in American Imaginaries* looks at the complex, often contradictory ways that slavery informs theorizations of national community in the region that has alternately been called the Black Atlantic, Greater Caribbean, or Postplantation Americas. Its transcolonial mapping takes as its cue studies of the political, psychological, and symbolic meanings of slavery initiated by Orlando Patterson's *Slavery and Social Death* (1982), Antonio Benitez-Rojo's *The Repeating Island* (1992), and Paul Gilroy's *The Black Atlantic* (1993). *The Masters and the Slaves* belongs to an emerging body of critical reappraisals of slavery and cultural and genetic hybridization in the Americas. But unlike Deborah Cohn's *Literature and Memory in the Two Souths* (1999), Timothy Cox's *Postmodern Tales of Slavery in the Americas* (2001), and George Handley's *Postslavery Literatures of the Americas* (2000), which focus on the novel, the majority of the essays that comprise this volume address "nonfictional" texts. They are also distinguished by their concern with the exclusionary implications of assimilationism—in particular, the ways that paradigms of *mestizaje* accommodate scientific racism and suppress contestatory forms of articulation. (In the title of this anthology—and frequently in this introduction—I employ *mestizaje* as a generic term for Caribbean paradigms of hybridity due to its currency in the United States as well as the sheer preeminence of Spanish.)

Through readings of essays, scientific writing, poetry, novels, literary criticism, memoires, and the visual arts from Brazil, Haiti, the United States, Puerto Rico, and Martinique, the contributors to *The Masters and the Slaves* look at topics such as the interface of homophobia with racial exclusion, the plantation as metaphor, the eroticization of the plantation economy, the relationship between texts that negotiate cultural versus biological models of *mestizaje*, and the resonance of nation-building narratives of interracial contact with contemporary models of hybridization. With the exception of Grosfoguel's and Subramanian's chapters, their studies were originally presented in a seminar of the same title at the Annual Meeting of the American Comparative Literature Association, a conference attended principally by scholars from U.S. institutions that took place in San Juan, Puerto Rico in April 2002. It is fitting that this project, concerned as it is with the clash between identity politics and Caribbean models of assimilation, originated in a locale—the meeting rooms of San Juan's Wyndham Condado Plaza overlooking the Atlantic Ocean—that is itself so heavily weighted with geopolitical symbolism. This *mise-en-scène* is underscored by Puerto Rico's enigmatic status as Free Associated State and as "island backyard" of the United States—indeed, in a Caribbean that, for Antonio Benítez-Rojo, is itself always constructed as a kind of plantation.

Despite the dialogical origins and development of American theorizations of slavery and race, studies that consider their implications in multiple cultural and linguistic contexts have frequently met with resistance. The territorial compartmentalization of the academy, together with the discordant interface between paradigms of hybridity and one-dropism, contribute to the problem of effectively addressing slavery from a post-plantation rather than national or shared language perspective. The result is that comparative studies produced in the United States tend to measure Latin American representations of race and slavery in relation to "normative" black/white dialectics. Alternately, they misinterpret exclusionary models of *mestizaje*, hybridity, and *créolité* as counter-discourses. In so doing, they themselves demonstrate how African/slave consciousness is absorbed and reified—in this case by the academy—so as to obfuscate the conflicted sociohistorical experience of enslavement and marginalization.

Two recent studies of the Caribbean novel raise a number of problems with postslavery scholarship—neocolonialist mappings of

"derivative" or inscrutable Caribbean discourses and uncritical interpretations of theories of hybridization—while at the same time par-
ticipating in the cross-dissemination of ideas about identity and,
therein, in the ongoing construction of "race" in the Americas:
Timothy J. Cox's *Postmodern Tales of Slavery in the Americas* (2001)
and Deborah H. Cohn's *History and Memory in the Two Souths*
(1999). In his introduction to *Postmodern Tales of Slavery in the
Americas*, a mostly theoretically sophisticated analysis of New World
slavery symbolics and master/slave dialogics, Cox laments the relative
absence in Latin America of a genre specific to the Anglo-North
American world. For Cox, the fact that there are "few written records
of slavery—slave narratives—in Latin America makes it difficult to do
comparative work" (xviii). Rather than look at the frequent incorporation and circumvention of black articulation in Iberian–American
polities, Cox suggests that the absence of an Afro-Hispanic movement
like the Harlem Renaissance or Negritude precludes an understanding
of how Afro-Hispanic aesthetics incorporate slavery. He chalks up
this phenomenon as an oddity not worth pursuing, as yet another
dimension of the enigma of race in Latin America:

> . . . .the variety among the Spanish-speaking nations makes it hard to
> generalize, plus people of African descent have never enjoyed a cen-
> tralized cultural and intellectual vogue, like the Harlem Renaissance or
> the Negritude movement, to get a group program started and
> developing. Furthermore, the dismal mid- and late-twentieth-century
> situations for blacks in Latin America tend to focus attention on the
> here and now rather than on the past. Two of the three novels written
> in Spanish that are discussed in this study, oddly enough, were
> composed by white males. (xiv)

In addition to Cox's claim that disparate conceptualizations of racial
authenticity and authorship impede rather than enrich scholarly work,
he ignores the ways that the Harlem Renaissance and Negritude were
informed by European and white American writers, publishers, readers,
and, indeed, by ethnography and *avant-garde* aesthetics. Cox sustains
the misguided premise—central to so many comparative studies—
that Latin America is the site of miscegenation and puzzling racial
"slippage" that are somehow unfathomable in the United States,
where the black/white dialectic is the normative model for understanding postslavery reality. One need look no further than the
Harlem Renaissance itself, to Langston Hughes's "I am your son,
white man!"[3] to unsettle the mythologized opposition between the

U.S. rigid color line and racially blurry Latin America and the Caribbean.

Cox's privileging of magical realism reveals a second problem with U.S. scholarship that celebrates what Nestor Garcia Canclini calls the "lazy, magical realist account for Latin American hybridity" (*Hybrid Cultures* 6). He identifies Alejo Carpentier's *El Reino de Este Mundo* as an exemplary "neo-slave narrative" that challenges metropolitan hegemony by situating the Haitian Revolution at the imaginative center of the postplantation American diaspora. Though Carpentier indeed indicts the terrors of colonization and enslavement, the problem is that *El Reino . . . .*'s most powerful lamentation is directed at the unending spiral of violence to befall the black nation in the lawless tropical periphery, beyond the reach of the civilizing European center—the literary equivalent of news media and scientific representations of the "third" or "non-world," where successive dictatorships and abrupt, violent regime change are constructed as intrinsically non-European and dissociated from sociopolitical cause and effect. The fact that so many scholars turn a blind eye to this text, in spite of Carpentier's insistence upon African mysticism, blacks' connection to nature and animals, and the chaotic, inevitable brutality of the ex-slave state, suggests a disinclination to hold Caribbean aesthetics to the same critical standards they would apply to "Western texts." Is this uncritical reading of Carpentier a guilty response to the historical dismissal of non-European aesthetics? Or, worse, is it due to a conceptualization of the Caribbean as a place where such sorts of black stereotypes are permissible, where racism suppressed in the metropolitan centers can find an outlet?

Deborah N. Cohn's *History and Memory in the Two Souths* (1999) reflects the same U.S.-centrism and praise for magical realism that weaken Cox's study. Rather than investigate the cross-circulation of race discourses, Cohn situates the U.S. South as the epicenter for the dissemination of narrative strategies for redemptive self-representation in relation to the victorious North. She is particularly interested in Faulkner's influence on the "decentering" narratives of the magical realists. Even if one were to accept the premise that Gabriel Garcia Marquez, Mario Vargas Llosa, and Alejo Carpentier articulate dissenting visions of Latin America that destabilize dominant discourse, Cohn's insistence that the U.S. South provided a voice for these writers effectively recenters them, aligning them in a peripheral relation to North America. Far more troubling are Cohn's even-handed indictment of the "materialism and commercialism" of the two norths (24) and her equation of the northern occupation of the

U.S. South with U.S. interventions in Hispano-America. Whereas one could productively join George Handley in conceptualizing the U.S. South as one of the first "colonies" of U.S. post-slavery imperial expansion (20),[4] Cohn's insistence upon the "double consciousness" (40) of the white writers she considers, together with her comparisons of Yankees with Yanquis and of the north with *el norte*, reflect a facile appropriation of black sociohistorical experience and social critique and a dangerously relativized geopolitics. She effectively collapses master/slave and north/south dialectics, placing white writers from both "souths" in the place of the ex-slave. Reversing the terms of this comparison, George Handley more effectively defines the relationship between master/slave and north/south: "Because U.S. imperialism imitates the very ideological structures of a colonial plantation discourse, one wonders if the South didn't win the Civil War" (25).

Notwithstanding problems with transnational slavery studies—the derivative positioning of Caribbean and Latin American discourses in relation to U.S. literary production, the uncritical celebration of *mestizaje* and the evaluation of non-U.S. conceptualizations of race according to one-dropism (unwittingly sustained as the normative gauge of identity)—a recent work challenges black/white, north/south dialectics in fiction, marketing, film, and sociology. In *Paradise and Plantation: Tourism and Culture in the Anglophone Caribbean* (2002), Ian Gregory Strachan shows how the advertising media "sell" the Caribbean as a relic of the lost world of slavery where the white visitor may leave behind the industrialized, postcapitalist world and enjoy a sense of slavery-era omnipotence in relation to Caribbean servants and beggars (106).[5] Strachan's reading of the marketing of slavery—the commodified black body, the eroticized plantation—elucidates sublimated desires attached to the pre-abolition/colonial era while pointing to the shifting signifiers of race when transported from the United States and Europe to the Bahaman resort.[6]

Like *Paradise and Plantation*, Barbara Browning's *Infectious Rhythm: Metaphors of Contagion and the Spread of African Culture* (1998) serves as a model for this volume's critique of hybridization discourses that reinforce colonialist dialectics. Browning problematizes the association of metaphysics with black political upheaval, and the emphasis upon "soul" that allows for the characterization of African culture as a "chaotic or uncontrolled force which can only be countered with military or police violence" (7). Browning's assertion that "This book begins—and ends—in Pelourinho" (16)—the Bahian neighborhood that was originally a slave auction site but has since been reappropriated as the heart of Afro-Brazilian cultural affirmation—points to another of *The Masters and the Slaves'* distinctions: its integration of Brazil into Caribbean and Atlantic Studies. Whereas Haiti has frequently been situated as the symbolic epicenter for black politicization, and Stuart Hall articulates the paradoxically key role of the postimperial United States in globally disseminated crosscurrents of black cultural production, Brazil has ordinarily been omitted from transnational literary and cultural analyses of slavery symbolics, despite the fact that that it represents the largest population of people of African descent outside of Africa, that it was home to the most formidable urban slave revolt and the largest and longest-standing maroon community in American history, and notwithstanding the key place of Brazil's "Racial Democracy" in global imaginaries for the last hundred years.

The linguistic gulf between Brazil and "Latin America" contributes to this omission, as does the challenge Brazil poses to identity politics paradigms that do not smoothly accommodate the rich ambivalences and contradictions surrounding race, power, citizenship, and the symbolic resonance of the plantation economy in Brazil. As indicated by the epigraph to this introduction, Africa is the privileged term in the construction of Brazilian national identity, yet that privilege relies on collapsing Africa with plantation-era systems of domination. After all, the country's international reputation consists in slaveryesque formulae such as the consummately festive spirit of its people, the sexual availability of its "racially mixed" women, and the physical prowess of its athletes—carnaval, the *mulata*, and soccer. This paradox has not been adequately challenged even or especially within Brazilian and Brazilianist academia. An example of the prevalence of this discourse is Caetano Veloso's recent CD, "Noites do Norte" (2000), wherein he invokes the invariably heroicized abolitionist Joaquim Nabuco—"slavery will for a long time remain the national characteristic of Brazil"—without anyone linking this passage to Nabuco's eugenically anxious lamentation, also in *O Abolicionismo* (1883), that slavery has "infiltrated the nation's veins," debilitating its evolutionary momentum.[7]

Because Brazilian assimilationism and "Racial Democracy" stand in such jarring contrast to U.S. segregationism and, later, to its race-based identity politics, they have provided material for a rich, if unnerving, body of comparative work in the social sciences. Studies from the late nineteenth century until the 1960s put forth the virtually uncontested idea that Brazil was a model for multicultural understanding to which the violent, intolerant United States should aspire.

On the other hand, Michael Hanchard's *Orpheus and Power* (1994) and Anthony W. Marx's *Making Race and Nation* (1998) typify the current critical tendency to overturn this pervasive "truth." Unfortunately, rather than investigate the paradoxically ubiquitous/ sublimated quality of blackness in Brazil, they emphasize the nation's deficiencies—its failure to battle for Civil Rights and to engage in race-based forms of contestation—as though these were the inevitable means for subverting unequal power relations independent of the sociohistorical contexts in which they emerge.

Timothy Cox's complaint about the relative absence in Latin America of slave narratives or of a black literary vanguard akin to the Harlem Renaissance resonates with Hanchard's analysis of Rio's black movement: whereas "the perverse silver lining" of segregation has been the "creation of self-sufficient institutions and collective proj- ects," he insists that Brazilian assimilationism clouds racial inequalities and impedes the development of sociohistorically based affiliations (83). In Marx's study of state-led race-making in South Africa, Brazil, and the United States, he argues that identity needs first to be fully developed in order that systems of domination may be destabilized. Unlike South Africa and the United States, Brazil's "diluted" racial conflicts (267) seem to lead to an aberrant cultural– political situation where "No comparable legal racial domination had been constructed to be reformed. . . . Instead, the lack of an official racial order that might have provoked stronger protest has left such discrimination largely unchanged" (270). Beyond sublimating the economic origins of colonialism and enslavement to the overarching paradigm of race, claims such as these seem to reflect the perception that the United States has been lucky not to experience the mind-numbing effects of Iberian assimilationism—as though the "fully developed" black/white dialectic in the United States were not also an illusion—and has thus come to a more informed, conscious understanding of the mecha- nisms of racial exploitation and the proper route to combating them.

Scholarship originating in the fields of literary and cultural studies—portending insight beyond discrediting the "myth" of Racial Democracy—is far rarer. Of the four chapters of this anthology on Brazil, three analyze Gilberto Freyre, the sociologist whose narrative of Brazilian culture privileges the plantation as the stage upon which the originary intermingling of Europeans and Africans took place— from whose synthesis, indeed, the nation's "uniqueness" and "cultural superiority" are said to derive.

In chapter 1, "The Sugar Daddy: Gilberto Freyre and the White Man's Love for Blacks," César Braga-Pinto traces the connection between racial exclusion and the sublimation of homosexuality in Freyre's work. Considering the interface of "democracy" with male friendship in *Casa-Grande e Senzala*, Braga-Pinto argues that the two concepts together define a national polity that erases the agency of blacks and gays. He shows how Freyre's preoccupation with white virility informs his displacement of sociohistorical mixed-race: in Freyre's work, the *mestizo* male is degenerated by interracial contact, whereas the genetic and cultural heritage of the slavery economy revives and increases the "potency" of white men. Braga-Pinto demystifies Freyre's insistence upon the "miscibility" of the Portuguese, credited for both their capacity for assimilating non-European cultures and for bisexuality. He poses the question, "How can one define the boundaries between racism and homophobia?" Ultimately, Braga-Pinto argues, in Western cultures (and particularly in those whose histories have been informed by colonialism and enslavement) there is no conception of interracial fraternity/friendship, with the result that interracial male relationships are consigned to the realm of the erotic. Homosexuality, like blackness, is acceptable only in the extent to which it is a transitory, evolutionary stage.

In chapter 2, "Writing Brazilian Culture," I analyze the impact of spatial dialectics on Freyre's model of symbolic *mestiçagem*. Because Freyre casts himself as a masterful subject who has equal domain in both elite and marginal sites, and because he conjoins that domain with his white socioeconomic identity, he displaces people of mixed African/European ancestry from the embodiment of hybridization and, therein, from the ability to represent the uniqueness of Brazilian culture. Through a reading of Freyre's essay, "Como e Porque Escrevi Casa-Grande e Senzala" (*How and Why I Wrote Casa-Grande e Senzala* 1968), I show that he claims free access to the black "underworld" while at the same time firmly locating himself in the plantation manor, the proper site for producing his "hybrid" text. I then situate this narrative in the context of "Reinterpring Alencar" (*Reinterpreting José de Alencar* 1962), an essay in which Freyre dismisses Machado de Assis on the grounds that he is "mulatto" and, thus, disabled from inhabiting and interpreting either term of the dialectic of Brazilian culture. Ultimately, I demonstrate that it is transcription—the master's or ethnographer's written rendering of hybridity—that Freyre conceptualizes as the mark of authentic Brazilian assimilationism.

Chapter 3 signals the transition to the U.S. slavery economy, conventionally conceived in opposition to Brazil's mythologized assimilation. In "Authority's Shadowy Double: Thomas Jefferson and the Architecture of Illegitimacy," Helena Holgersson-Shorter destabilizes the premise of fixed racial oppositions on U.S. plantations. She takes us from the northeastern Brazilian plantation manor to Thomas Jefferson's notorious Virginia estate, Monticello, to address the defamiliarizing place of the mulatto in the U.S. racial imaginary. Holgersson-Shorter considers Jefferson's definition of albinos as "white blacks" whom he substitutes for his own unmentionable "white slave" offspring. She theorizes Jefferson's writing about albinos "as a metaphoric paradigm for mulatto representation in American culture and literature" (21) and addresses the ways that the mulatto family hidden within Monticello contributes to the instability of his narrative voice in *Notes on the State of Virginia* (1782). Holgersson-Shorter shows how, through a quasi-Freyrean move complicated by the particular quality of U.S. anxiety about miscegenation, Jefferson intermittently situates himself in the place of the mulatto, succumbing to precisely the recessive traits he attributes to the albinos.

Though all of the chapters implicitly engage with the threat of revolt, chapter 4 directly addresses the Haitian Revolution, the ultimate sign of black uprising that has reverberated throughout the Americas for the last two centuries. In "Race, Nation and the Symbolics of Servitude in Haitian *Noirisme*," Valerie Kaussen explores the representation of modernity, slavery, and revolution in the nationalist movement that developed in the 1920s and 1930s as a response to the U.S. occupation of Haiti (1915–1934). Through close readings of the ethnographic writings of Haiti's premier *noiriste* theorists—Lorimer Denis and François "Papa Doc" Duvalier—she shows how they conceptualize slavery as that which is most authentically Haitian. Where Gilberto Freyre insists upon slaveholders' embodiment of "black hopes and fears" to produce them as the ultimate hybrids, for Denis and Duvalier, national unity rests upon a conceptualization of the state as the incarnation of both the rebellious slave and the master who keeps his chaotic energy in check. Exploring connections between the slavery discourses of Cuba and Haiti, Kaussen then turns to Maurice Casseus's *Viejo* (1935) to explain his repoliticization of the "black slave" image, reconnecting the sign of the "Haitian Revolution" with class conflict and refiguring the "Sugar plantation as the space of a transnational movement of resistance" (14).

Chapter 5 weaves the plantation into an examination of urban architecture as colonial mapping of center and periphery. It also introduces Frantz Fanon into a discussion that has thus far been marked by inquiries into dominant discourse. In "Fanon as 'Metrocolonial'

Flaneur in the Caribbean Post-Plantation/Algerian Colonial City,"
Nalini Natarajan considers Fanon "As a transnational activist who
moved between two colonies, (thus altering) the reference point for
the study of colonialism, traditionally the metropolis" (4). She looks
at the impact of his Caribbean origins on his theorization of Algeria
and at how his exposure to Algeria informs his interpretation of
Martinique. Reading Fanon's representations of urban landscapes in
*Wretched of the Earth* (1961) and *Black Skin, White Masks* (1952),
Natarajan poses a series of questions: How does the master/slave
dialectic of New World plantation ideology translate to notions of city
space? How do the colonized react to the appropriation of their
subjectivity by the colonizers/racially dominant? Does the built
environment of the city suggest new models for understanding the
master/slave dialectic, and for altering systems of domination?
Natarajan's analysis of the relationship of architecture to the plantation-
derived racial dialectics master/slave and white/black engages with
Holgersson-Shorter's critique of Jefferson's "scientific" and architectural modes of dissimulation, my study of Freyre's seigniorial incorporation of blackness within the *casa-grande*, and Jossiana Arroyo's
interpretation of "tropicalist" mappings in chapter 5.

In "From the Tropics: Cultural Subjectivity and Politics in
Gilberto Freyre," Arroyo analyzes Freyre's *tropicalismo*, a theory
crystallized with the publication of *New World in the Tropics* in 1959,
and informed by northeastern Brazilian conceptualizations of masculinity, eugenics, and civilization, together with European binaries of
tropical degeneracy and exuberance. She addresses the problem of
reappropriating theoretical frameworks like *tropicalismo* and transculturation in U.S. humanities and social sciences, where the "local"
arguments are lost. In addition to looking at the impact of theories of
assimilation, and of Freyrean *tropicalismo* in particular, on Latin
American, Caribbean, and Latino Studies, Arroyo investigates the
global transnationalism originally inscribed within the theories
themselves, situating them in the context of U.S. postcolonial interventions in the Caribbean in the 1960s and the desire of Caribbean
elites such as Freyre to negotiate their relationship to the United
States in the Cold War world.

Ramón Grosfoguel also interrogates the relationship of Caribbean
mappings to contemporary geopolitics. In chapter seven, "Hybridity
and *Mestizaje*: Syncretism or Subversive Complicity? Subalternity
from the Perspective of the Coloniality of Power," his premise is that
the "independence" of third world nations has not been effective in
reversing the flow of capital from South to North; evidence of the

inadequacy of "third world nationalism" is the fact that in Carribbean countries like Puerto Rico, which did not attain independence, metropolitan citizenship affords transferences of wealth from North to South that do not occur in the independent nations. Grosfoguel evaluates hybridity and *mestizaje* in this context, showing how postmodernists who interpret these processes as "syncretic" perpetuate the same Eurocentricsm that led Spanish colonizers to view slaves' praying to Catholic saints as evidence of Christianization. He urges a reevaluation of these political–cultural strategies—tactics that are like the silent undercurrent of the "clave," Africanizing hegemonic music without making itself noticed—from the subaltern side of colonial difference. Grosfoguel points to oppositional movements of "subversive complicity"—from Martin Luther King and Aimé Cesaire to the Zapatistas and the Madres de Mayo—as the most apt tactics in a world in which there is no "outside" of the West.

In chapter 8, "The Rhythm of Macumba: Lívio Abramo's Engagement with Afro-Brazilian Culture," Luiza Franco Moreira brings us back to the original stage for this collection. She looks at how a writer and an artist with discordant political positions collaborated in constructing images of Brazilians as the mixed-race "people of the future." Cassiano Ricardo, a poet and journalist, was committed to the authoritarian and repressive regime led by Getúlio Vargas (1937–1945), while Lívio Abramo, the artist who illustrated the first edition of Ricardo's *Marcha para Oeste* [Westward March], was sympathetic with the socialist opposition to the dictatorship. By exploring the interplay between Ricardo's and Abramo's texts, Moreira elucidates the political position underlying Abramo's work and shows how he employs his illustrations to parody or place the ideology of the written text in quotes. Her discussion of the first edition of *Marcha para Oeste* makes it possible to recover not only the conflicts that marked the cultural and political life of Brazil in the 1940s but also the key role that varying accounts of miscegenation played in this nation's imaginary.

The final chapter of *The Masters and the Slaves* bridges a gap between critical theory and poetic meditations on race in the Americas. In "Blood, Memory, and Nation: Massacre and Mourning in Edwidge Danticat's *The Farming of Bones*," Shreerekha Subramanian considers David Eng's formulation of the normative melancholia of the dispossessed in relation to Edwidge Danticat's narrative of the 1937 massacre of Haitians in the Dominican Republic in *The Farming of Bones* (1998). With the nationalist erasure of blackness, whiteness becomes a contagion that places the other in an endless condition of mourning: Subramanian considers Danticat's characters' imagined community with the dead as an act of political empowerment, their fluency in the language of death a refusal to relinquish that which was stolen away.

From maroon to postcapitalist migration, from plantation manor to metrocolonial "center," the essays that follow look at master/slave symbolics in relation to agency, aesthetics, and ethnographic science. With their inquiry into discourses of inclusion that sustain systems of subordination, they also suggest a point of departure for rethinking displays of geopolitical might not overtly related to the post-plantation.[8] How can we begin to theorize contemporary empire in relation to the African enslavement that nurtured Western capitalism and, eventually, gave rise to U.S. hegemony? While a study of the resonance of slavery aesthetics with contemporary empire building is beyond the scope of this anthology, I would like to suggest that future studies consider parallels between representations of the "negro problem" and the "Arab mind," fear of the dissemination of Haitian slave revolt across the Americas and anxiety about Arab incursions across U.S. and European borders, eugenic anxiety and the discourse of terrorist "cells." What connections can be drawn between fear of black politicization in the Americas and the fear of mounting resistance to the U.S.-Anglo Empire? Or between the orientalizing representational practices employed to keep Africans, then the "East," at bay?[9]

## NOTES

1. This and all other translations of Gilberto Freyre are mine. *Casa-Grande e Senzala* literally means *The Plantation Manor and the Slave Barracks* though it was translated into English as *The Masters and the Slaves* (1946).

2. Upon receiving an honorary doctorate from the University of Las Villas in 1959, Ché Guevara issues this entreaty to the "proprietors of the University" and, implicitly, to the Cuban national community (Retamar, 45).

3. See "Mulatto," in *The Collected Poems of Langston Hughes*, Arnold Rampersad, ed. New York: Random House, 1994.

4. Lois Parkinson Zamora is the first to theorize the shared histories of colonization, slavery, and defeat by the "North" that link the U.S. south with Spanish America (see Zamora, *The Usable Past*, 1997).

5. Strachan complicates this picture by scrutinizing the posture of the black visitor to the Caribbean who "indulges in playing the role of the white man or woman in the tropics" (17), and situates this role-playing in relation to popular media production such as Terry

MacMillan's narrative of a wealthy professional's sexual rebirth with her nineteen-year-old Jamaican lover in *How Stella Got Her Groove Back* (1996) and Eddie Murphy's spoof in "Raw" (1987) of "Dexter," the prototypical ". . . . Caribbean man (who) is supposedly beast-like, the object of sexual fantasy, the site of devious promiscuity" (16). Future studies of African American representations of the Caribbean could address Michael Jackson's controversial portraits of the Rio *favela*, "Dona Marta," and of the Bahian neighborhood, Pelourinho, in "They Don't Care About Us" (Spike Lee, 1996).

6. Ian Strachan also makes the important connection between human and non-human othering, the rhetorical operations whereby aliens of all kinds are "cast in natural terms." He discusses rationalizations for plantation slavery in relation to the "doctrine of human uniqueness," the Cartesian conceptualization of "animals as machines incapable of reason and perhaps even sensation" (18) and "Aristotle's outlook on slaves, horses, and oxen—all equivalents in his view: inanimate and animate tools" (18).

7. For a discussion of the eugenic undercurrents of Brazilian abolitionism, see David Haberly, "Abolitionism in Brazil: Anti-Slavery and Anti-Slave," *Luso-Brazilian Review* 9.2 (1972) and Alexandra Isafahni-Hammond, "Joaquim Nabuco's Black Mandate," *Hispania* (2002).

8. One of the richest representations of the interface between black/white politics in the U.S. and contemporary empire building is the role played by Denzel Washington as the head of the FBI terrorism task force in the film *The Seige* (1998). Casting the agent for the suppression of "radical Islam" as a black man, *The Seige* justifies the internment and torture of men of Middle Eastern descent. Another text worth investigating is Spike Lee's theorization of slavery era motifs in the entertainment industry in "Bamboozled" (2001). A particularly rich moment is when the television producer, played by Michael Rappaport, instructs the scriptwriter, played by Damon Wayans, that he doesn't want the show to take place in a housing project: "No gold teeth, none of that shit.... 'Mantan's New Millenium Minstrel Show' is going to take place on a plantation." As a counterpoint to Lee's nuanced take on racial parody in "Bamboozled," it is important to attend to his insensitivity to the parallels between racial exploitation within the nation's borders and the subjugation of non-world peoples outside those borders. Lee's shortsighted take on race and power is captured by his 1999 Navy video ad, "Jamming Sailors," whose purpose he claims is to ". . . show sailors in jazz and rock bands, portraying a creative and fun slice of Navy life" (Norm Dixon, "Spike Lee Does the Right Thing for Imperialism," 1999).

9. In addition to Frantz Fanon's classic discussion of the veil in relation to negritude (*A Dying Colonialism*, 1970), those interested in situating African enslavement in the context of contemporary incursions in

the Middle East could consider Orlando Patterson's *Freedom: Freedom in the Making of Western Culture* (1991) and Edward Said's theorization of libratory discourse in relation to efforts to correct Arab "degeneration" (see, e.g., "Orientalism: Twenty-five Years Later," 2003). João José Reis's study of the Malê Revolt, organized by Moslem slaves and ex-slaves in 1835 in Bahia, Brazil, provides a paradigm not only for linking post-plantation studies to the East/West "culture clash" but also for upsetting the construct of blind Moslem abeyance to authority (*Slave Rebellion in Brazil*, 1993). Islam has, of course, been harnessed—in albeit problematic ways—as a shield against white on black racism in the United States by the Nation of Islam. "Intifada" has been employed in relation to the L.A. uprising of 1992 (Goldberg, 105). And the Recifean favela, "Iraque," uses its name to connect poverty and racial inequality in the Brazilian northeast with U.S. imperialism in the Middle East. (This geopolitical connection is redoubled by "Iraque's" location just south of another *favela* called "Vietnam," which by turn resonates with the Rio de Janeiro slum, "Koréia.")

## Works Cited

Benítez-Rojo, Antonio. *The Repeating Island: The Caribbean and the Postmodern Perspective*, 2d. ed. Durham: Duke University Press, 1996.

Browning, Barbara. *Infectious Rhythm: Metaphors of Contagion and the Spread of African Culture*. New York: Routledge, 1998.

Cox, Timothy. *Postmodern Tales of Slavery in the Americas*. New York: Garland, 2001.

Cohn, Deborah. *History and Memory in the Two Souths: Recent Southern and Spanish American Fiction*. Nashville: Vanderbilt University Press, 1999.

Fanon, Frantz. *A Dying Colonialism*. Trans. Haakon Chevalier. London: Pelican, 1970.

Freyre, Gilberto. *Casa-Grande e Senzala*. Rio de Janeiro: José Olympio, 1984.

García Canclini, Nestor. *Hybrid Cultures: Strategies for Leaving and Entering Modernity*. Minneapolis: University of Minnesota Press, 1995.

Gilroy, Paul. *The Black Atlantic: Modernity and Double Consciousness*. Cambridge: Harvard University Press, 1993.

Hanchard, Michael. *Orpheus and Power: The Movimento Negro of Rio de Janeiro and São Paulo, Brazil, 1945–1988*. Princeton: Princeton University Press, 1994.

Handley, George. *Postslavery Literatures in the Americas: Family Portraits in Black and White*. Charlottesville: University Press of Virginia, 2000.

Marx, Anthony W. *Making Race and Nation: A Comparison of the United States, South Africa and Brazil*. Cambridge: Cambridge University Press, 1998.

Reis, João José. *Slave Rebellion in Brazil: The Muslim Uprising of 1835 in Bahia*. Baltimore: Johns Hopkins University Press, 1993.

Retamar, Roberto Fernández. *Caliban and other Essays.* Minneapolis: University of Minnesota Press, 1989.

Strachan, Ian. *Paradise and Plantation: Tourism and Culture in the Anglophone Caribbean.* Charlottesville: University of Virginia Press, 2002.

Veloso, Caetano. *Noites do Norte.* São Paulo: Universal Music Ltda, 2000.

Zamora, Lois Parkinson. "The Usable Past: The Idea of History in Modern U.S. and Latin American Fiction." *Do the Americas Have a Common Literature?* Ed. Gustavo Pérez Firmat. Durham: Duke University Press, 1990.

# The Sugar Daddy: Gilberto Freyre and the White Man's Love for Blacks

*César Braga-Pinto*

This chapter addresses representations of homosexuality in the work of the writer and sociologist Gilberto Freyre (1900–1987), particularly in relation to his notions of racial contact and miscegenation. By looking at the configuration of "homosocial desires" in some of Freyre's most important texts, one can begin to understand the role played by narratives of interracial and homosexual relationships in the structuring of what Freyre himself called the "Brazilian patriarchal family" and, therefore, in the canonical representation of Brazil as a *mestizo* nation. I first discuss Freyre's view of the always ambivalent nature of the Portuguese colonizers, an ambivalence that expresses itself not only in racial but also in sexual terms. I then discuss how he employs a particular notion of democratic society, based on traditional views of male *friendship*, to define the boundaries of the relations between the races and to construct an image of Brazil that ultimately erases the political agency of Africans and Afro-Brazilians and, at the same time, of homosexuals.

## COLONIAL AMBIVALENCES

Freyre's hybrid sociological work, *Casa Grande e Senzala* (written in 1933 and translated in 1946 as *The Masters and the Slaves*), was one of the first attempts to think of Brazil as a multiracial/multicultural society and to cast *mestizaje* in positive terms. Freyre spent most of his life interpreting the relationship between the Portuguese and other peoples, l created a narrative in which the Portuguese colonizer appears tolerant, flexible or, as he often writes, *plastic*. For Freyre, the Portuguese are characterized by "miscibility," or the capacity to adapt to other regions, climates, and cultures. In the 1950s, such ideas were crystallized in a notion called "lusotropicalism," or the unique ability of the Portuguese to acclimate to the tropics. These ideas were subsequently appropriated by the Portuguese dictator, Salazar—of whom Freyre was an admirer—to justify Portuguese colonialism in Africa.

*The Masters and the Slaves* traces the Brazilian heritage to the encounter between Portuguese, Africans, and Indigenous peoples in the sugar cane plantation society of the first centuries of Brazilian colonization. In spite of his attempt to celebrate miscegenation, Freyre presents interracial relations as the cause of certain historical aberrations, and in several instances he associates racial contact with degeneration and disease. Such is the case in a passage of the first chapter of *The Masters and the Slaves*, when Freyre struggles to dissociate miscegenation from contagion by means of a convoluted argument:

> . . . . The advantage of miscegenation in Brazil ran parallel to the tremendous disadvantage of syphilis. These two factors began operating at the same time: one to form the Brazilian, the ideal type of modern man for the tropics, a European with *Negro or Indian blood* to revive his energy; the other to deform him. Out of this there arises a certain confusion of thought on the subject of responsibilities, many attributing to miscegenation effects that are chiefly due to syphilis, the Negro or the Amerindian or even the Portuguese race being held responsible for the "ugliness" and "ignorance" of those of our backland populations who have been most affected by syphilis or eaten with worms, whereas the truth is that each one of these races, in a pure or uncrossed state, is exhausted with producing admirable examples of beauty and physical robustness. (my emphasis, 70–71)

According to Freyre, colonization had advantages and disadvantages, but miscegenation should be understood for its positive value as a dimension of "civilization." This means that the ideal man for the tropics is a European whose energy has been revived by contact with Africans and Indigenous peoples. "Good" miscegenation is the nourishment of European civilization with Indian and African *blood*—an ambiguous term that conflates the meanings of genetic and cultural heritage contained in miscegenation with a history of violence and sacrificial death.

In contrast to this "good" miscegenation that is synonymous with civilization, Freyre reintroduces the threat of physical degradation via miscegenation and attributes this to the effects of syphilis or, in his playful language, to *syphilization*. Although Freyre suggests that, contrary to general opinion, Europeans were the ones who introduced syphilis to the New World, he frequently underscores that the Portuguese man or boy contracted syphilis through sexual intercourse with black and indigenous Brazilians. Though racial mixture may not be the cause of syphilis, interracial sexual contact remains the context that explains how Brazilian society was both formed and de-formed. Thus, syfillization, which above all characterizes the *mestizo* man from the hinterland, is the negative side of civilization, that is to say, of true miscegenation—which, I repeat, means European culture "energized" by African or Indigenous "blood." In other words, even if Freyre intends to celebrate the African and Indigenous heritage of Brazil, this heritage is always ambivalent, and the resulting picture oscillates between the symbolic and the genetic. At the same time that Freyre suggests that the *mestizo* male may have degenerated as the result of a history of racial contact (represented by his syphilization), he suggests that the genetic and cultural heritage resulting from the sugar cane plantation economy has revived the energy and increased the potency of the white man.

In another suggestive and ambivalent passage, Freyre discusses the consequences of labor division in plantation society, and concludes that its outcome was as follows:

> Each white master at the manor was left with two left hands, and each black man with two right hands . . . The white man's body became almost exclusively a membrum virile. He now had the hands of a woman, the feet of a boy and only his sex became arrogant and virile. In contrast to the blacks—many of them were enormous giants, but their weanies were those of little boys. (429, my translation)

To be sure, Freyre's metaphorical explanation is meant to suggest that plantation society exploited the black's physical labor, making the white man inept for it. Here and elsewhere, Freyre intends to demonstrate both the good and evil results of a colonization based on slave labor and the plantation economy. He wants to counter earlier evolutionist and eugenicist theories which claimed that racial contact and miscegenation were a source of degeneration, thus justifying any negative result of racial mixture in historical rather than genetic terms. On the one hand, he emphasizes an original kinship or symbiosis between whites and blacks; on the other hand, as we see from the androgynous and Frankenstein-like figures, which he imagines as the legacy of the plantation economy, Freyre once again deploys a rhetoric that associates racial contact with the threat of physical degeneration—even though one might argue that the body is presented as a metaphor for society as a whole. Furthermore, Freyre's insistence upon the contrast between the sizes of blacks' and whites' genitalia suggests not only a contact that is essentially sexual but, even more importantly, a relationship that is fundamentally asymetrical. If, as Freyre will later suggest, miscegenation is a form of interpenetration between white men and blacks, it is needless to call attention to the way in which some may be more deeply penetrated than others.

As early as the first pages of *The Masters and the Slaves*, Freyre somewhat unexpectedly associates the pre-colonial history of Portugal and the supposed Portuguese inclination to miscegenation with, if not homosexuality, at least bisexuality. Freyre insists upon the notion of the "relaxed flexibility" of the Portuguese as well as their tendency toward a "balance of antagonisms." He attributes these characteristics to their unique geographical and historical situation of "bi-continentalism," which he compares with "bisexualism:"

> In its ethnic and cultural indeterminateness between Europe and Africa, Portugal appears to have been always the same as other portions of the peninsula. A species of bi-continentalism that, in a population so vague and ill-defined, corresponds to bisexuality in the individual. It would be difficult to imagine a people more fluctuating than the Portuguese, the feeble balance of antagonisms reflected in everything that pertains to them, conferring upon them an easy and relaxed flexibility that is at times disturbed by grievous hesitations, along with a special wealth of aptitudes that are frequently discrepant and hard to reconcile for the purpose of useful expression or practical initiative. (7)

Freyre thus claims that, for historical reasons, the Portuguese were not race-conscious and therefore could not have been racists in the same way the Anglo-Saxons were in North America. But what I find rather intriguing is that Freyre blatantly associates the *ethnic* ambivalence of the Portuguese with *sexual* flexibility and ambivalence. If we read carefully, it seems that Freyre is suggesting that bisexuality—not androgyny, as one might expect—like racial "indeterminateness," is a specifically Portuguese inclination—and a positive one! Are we to conclude that, for Freyre, the Portuguese were not gender-conscious and, for this reason, that they were disinclined to homophobia?

The fact is that when Freyre discusses the early history of the African heritage in Brazil he often describes the relationship between the white master and the black slave in sexual terms. The black man is often the central object and partner in the white boy's sexual initiation—which for Freyre only confirms Portuguese virility and disposition toward sex, since the black man is often represented in a feminine role. As early as 1928 (in his *Manifesto Regionalista*), Freyre celebrated African "contributions" to the culture of Portuguese descendents by feminizing the image of black men. In his reading, the black man does not antagonize the white man; on the contrary, he willingly cooperates and even serves him in all senses, sometimes at the table, sometimes behind the bushes. Freyre defines the Portuguese as gluttonous boys and men (*Manifesto Regionalista*, 69) who are "always ready, in a Franciscan-like manner, to fraternize ("confraternizar") with their brown ("pardos") and black brothers;" for Freyre, this would explain "the growing Amerindian and African influence over the colonizer's food and sweets ("mesa e sobremesa"), due to the mediation not only of indigenous girls ("cunhãs") and "negras minas," but also of male cooks or "mestre-cucas": generally big and effeminate black men, or big black sissies" ('pretalhões amaricados,' 68).

Thus, even if Freyre writes in terms of black and white "fraternal relations," the colonial interracial penetration he imagines can hardly be called a form of brotherly love. In fact, Freyre explicitly discusses the social and sexual exchanges between blacks and whites in terms of a sadomasochism inherent to the history of the colonial encounter—that which Freyre calls "master sadism" ('sadismo de senhor') and the corresponding "slave masochism" ("masoquismo de escravo") (*CGS*, 51). Yet in spite of this apparent violence, the interracial encounter turns out to be complementary rather than antagonistic. Ultimately, the "balance of antagonisms" which Freyre repeatedly defines as the essence of the *formação brasileira* (Brazilian upbringing) consists of a harmonious balance between the sadism of the elites and the masochism of the masses, the latter of whom rarely revolt and even then only in sacrificial, messianic movements (51).

Thus, in order to understand racial democracy and lusotropicalism, one must look not only at how *mestizaje* results from relations between Portuguese men and African and Indigenous women, but also at how, according to Freyre, a particular form of homosociability is articulated in the tropics, that is, in the colonial setting. In the next section, I discuss Freyre's conceptualization of homosocial relations in general (i.e. within the same ethnic group), and the manner in which the inclusion of blacks disrupts the image of a society constituted by bonds of friendship and fraternity. In his attempt to represent a fraternal, multiracial society, Freyre ultimately conflates a number of anxieties and taboos, in particular those concerning racial contact, homosexuality, and incest.

## THE WHITE MAN AND HIS BLACK BROTHER

It is not only in the American novel that the noblest meaning of the term friendship has been traditionally understood as a *spiritual* relationship between *men*. In his well-known essay, "Of Friendship," Michel de Montaigne (1533–1592) claims that women "in no instance ha[ve] yet succeeded in attaining it, and by the common agreement of the ancient schools [are] excluded from it" (138). For Montaigne, true friendship should be an "alliance of brotherhood" that "feeds on communication" (136). He understands it as a "harmony of wills" (137) or as a "fusion of wills" (141); in contrast to the kinship between father and son, or that "other, licentious Greek love [which] is justly abhorred by our morality" (138), Montaigne defines true friendship as of a "more equitable and equable kind" (139). The (homosexual) love of the Greeks, he argues, cannot be defined as friendship because, on the one hand, it involved "a necessary disparity in age and [such] a difference in the lovers' functions;" moreover, it "was simply founded on external beauty, the false image of corporeal generation" (138). For Montaigne, friendship has to be based on something other than physical appearance, while at the same time involving a certain equality of status or equilibrium of forces between the two parties.

In *Politiques de l'amitié*, the French philosopher Jacques Derrida argues that not only the Western notion of friendship has traditionally been founded on the concept of fraternity, but also that our notions of democracy, and even humanity, are modeled on such terms. As Derrida traces the canonization of the Western concept of friendship as the representation of *brotherly* love, he asks the following questions: "How did it exclude the feminine or heterosexuality, the friendship between women or friendship between a man and a woman? Why can't we find any essential account of female or heterosexual experiences of friendship? Why such a heterogeneity between *eros* and *philía*?" (my translation, 308).

Neither Montaigne nor Derrida discuss the place of race or ethnicity in the definition or canonization of friendship, but we could add the following questions: How has friendship, understood as brotherly love, excluded that other fundamental historical heterogeneity, namely, racial (and perhaps also ethnic) difference? Hasn't the construction of the relationship between black and white men been conceived (in the Western tradition) as parallel to the heterosexual relationship and, therefore, as asymmetrical and unable to constitute "true friendship," at least in societies whose history is characterized by colonialism and slavery? If Western representations of the relationship between black and white men have often been sexualized (as if since that relationship cannot constitute a form of *philía* it necessarily enters the realm of *éros*), how can one define, in modern multiracial societies, the boundaries between racism and homophobia? If democracy is understood in terms of friendship and brotherly love, how can one interpret the famous expression "*racial* democracy" that has been associated with Freyre's ideas?[1] Is it really possible to imagine a non-consanguineous model of friendship/brotherhood? Is the notion of Brazil as a "racial democracy" truly multiracial and multicultural?

Leslie Fiedler was probably the first literary critic to discuss the intersections between homosexuality and race in the North American novel. In a seminal article that is nonetheless little known outside the field of American Studies, he suggests that the construction of "a national myth of masculine love" in the United States is contradicted by both the actual existence of homosexual love and by the unstable relationship between white and black men in American society. The chastity and innocence of this imagined love, which is always superior to the vulgar representation of heterosexual love is, according to Fiedler, one of the foundational American myths. He argues that, from Mark Twain's *Huckleburry Finn* to Herman Melville's *Moby Dick* and beyond, the representation of love among males is at the center of the American novel.

This is a form of love that is certainly physical, but that cannot be called sexual only because it is protected by a certain "childlike ignorance" (Fiedler, 7). Furthermore, in blatant contradiction to the reality of American society, in American classic fiction this masculine love takes place between a white and a brown or black man. This fictional love, which Fiedler calls "the profound dream of love in our relation to the Negro" (8), is all the more superior to heterosexual love for black women because, though interracial, it will never lead to miscegenation: "So long as there is no mingling of blood, soul may couple with soul in God's undefiled forest" (9). According to the American critic, this is more than a dream of reconciliation; it is the desire for full acceptance, beyond guilt or the need for forgiveness: the black or brown man "will comfort us, as if our offence against him were long ago remitted, were never truly *real*" (11). Fiedler concludes that "Behind the white American's nightmare that someday, no longer tourist, inheritor, or liberator, he will be rejected, refused, he dreams of his acceptance at the breast he has most utterly offended. It is a dream so sentimental, so outrageous, so desperate, that it redeems our concept of boyhood from nostalgia to tragedy" (11).

I do not intend (and it is not within my capacity) to discuss the limits of Fiedler's interpretation of the U.S. literary imagination, though I find the terms of his discussion enlightening.These terms have only recently become the central concerns of literary and queer studies. In particular, Fiedler anticipates notions such as "the homosocial continuum" and "homosexual panic," coined by American critic Eve Sedgwick in *Between Men: English Literature and Male Homosocial Desire*, wherein she proposes that "to draw the 'homosocial' back into the orbit of 'desire,' of the potentially erotic, then, is to hypothesize the potential unbrokenness of a continuum between homosocial and homosexual—a continuum whose visibility, for men, in our society, is radically disrupted" (1–2). Along the same lines, Fiedler suggests that to call love among males sexual would be like the "profanation of a dream" (9). I believe that Fiedler's insights, like Sedwick's theoretical articulation of homosocial desires, can shed new light on the representation of interracial friendship and homosexual love in Brazilian literature. More specifically, I would argue that by looking at the more or less tenuous breaks in "the homosocial continuum," one can better understand the processes of redefining and renegotiating categories of race and class that were taking place in Brazil during the 1930s.

By contrast with Fiedler's interpretation of American literature, what is striking in Brazilian fiction is that relationships between white and black men are not simply conceived as innocent. Adolfo Caminha's (1867–1897) *O Bom Crioulo*, written as early as 1896, is considered the first novel ever to place homosexual love—a homosexual relationship between a black man and a white man—at its center. Whereas the U.S. interracial male couple conceals a familiar fear of miscegenation, in post-Freyrean Brazil such anxiety is said not to exist; on the contrary, racial mixture is celebrated, often as a panacea for the tensions and contradictions inherited from a history of colonialism and slavery. To better understand the role of the interracial male couple in Freyre's work, one must first look at how homosocial relations have been represented (in general as well as in Freyre) in the context of somewhat homogeneous communities, that is to say, within ethnic or racial groups.

In *The Masters and the Slaves*, Freyre discusses the role of fraternal bonding in the constitution of communities. In a section on indigenous "contributions" to Brazilian society, he describes certain primitive forms of masculine sociability—which he terms "homomixia"—among the *Bororo*. This form of sociability, he writes, is manifest in the interior of secret male societies that the Bororo called "baito." According to Freyre, the purpose of these societies, which occurred "naturally, and without the feeling of sinful act" (118), was to "affirm the prestige of the male over the female" (118). Although such societies were intended to reinforce fraternal bonds, Freyre points out that these bonds were always potentially sexual: "The affinities which were praised were fraternal ones, from man to man; that is, virile affection. The result was an environment favorable to homosexuality" (136). "Homomixia," then, is a homosocial space where individuals (of the same sex and from the same social or ethnic group—in other words, "brothers") reinforce their social bonds by emphasizing their privileges over women (and perhaps also over other men), a practice that is always potentially (homo)sexual. Freyre seems to articulate a potential and perhaps desirable continuity of male relations, though he does not quite challenge the homophobic interdictions and taboos that structure Western patriarchal societies.

The boundaries between *homosexual acts* and *homosocial pacts* are indeed one of Freyre's favorite topics. In his diaries—which he claims to have written during his adolescence, beginning at age fifteen—he refers to homosexuality a number of times. In an entry in 1922 in Oxford (he was then about twenty-one years old), he gives the following, rather ambivalent testimony about his memory of what is in fact a "nonevent" or an event that never took place: "I now remember that in my college boy days I never had a homosexual experience. I was almost an angel. I would have been an angel except for solitary and reciprocal masturbation—which I rarely practiced" (my translation, *Tempo Morto e Outros Tempos*, 104). Later, Freyre suggests that he witnessed (if not experienced) homosexual behavior in his travels to Oxford and Berlin:

> In Oxford, young men dancing with young men is not rare . . . these are dances which sometimes end up in kissing and hugging. The truth, however, is that such outbursts are perhaps not that frequent here as they are in post-war Germany. There, the myth of the "race of the masters" corresponds to much of the sexual masochism on the part of the young Germans, the most seigniorial of whom seem to be delighted to be hurt by brown and exotic men. In Oxford, what one finds is, rather, the inclination to intense friendships between young men similar to those which existed—I suppose—among the platonic Greeks. They may eventually have something homosexual to them. But it is almost

always—this is how it appears to me—a transitory homosexuality, without the consummation which in Recife gave fame to the extremely intelligent and cultivated consul of S.M.B., Mr. D. (102–103)

Rather than speculate about Freyre's actual sexual orientation, what interests me is the contrast he establishes between German sexual acts with brown and exotic men—which reproduce master–slave dynamics while simultaneously turning them upside down—and British (or Greek) male sociability, which coincides with Montaigne's brotherly love, a love that should be mostly (but not exclusively) spiritual. In other words, just as in Bororo homosocial societies, even if these fraternal relationships do become physical, this should be occasional and by no means become a habit or define a form of asymmetrical, master–slave relationship. Such forms of "transitory homosexuality" are acceptable as long as their purpose is to teach and reinforce the fraternal bonds of men of the same racial, ethnic, or cultural background and to stress the exclusion of women from the masculine social space. The German homosexual acts are understood as a form of perversion, not only because they are asymmetrical, but most importantly because they reverse top/bottom, masculine/ feminine, and master/slave oppositions—ultimately, because they define not only practices but identities as well.

The distinction between friendship (which may include transitory homosexuality) and pederasty is the central theme of Freyre's two novels, *Dona Sinhá e o Filho Padre* (1964, translated as *Mother and Son, a Brazilian Tale*, 1967) and its sequel, *O Outro Amor do Dr. Paulo* (*Dr. Paulo's Other Love*, 1977). Both novels depict the relationship between a white youngster, androgynously named José Maria, and his *mestizo* friend, Paulo Tavares. Rather than analyze these works, I prefer to cite the readings proposed by Jossianna Arroyo in her essay, "Brazilian Homoerotics," wherein she relates "the cultural reconciliation of opposites in Brazilian culture" to Freyre's notion of "bisexual writing" (61). According to Arroyo, Freyrean "cultural subjectivity is based on this homosocial alliance that erases racial lines to build a 'national brotherhood' " (62), which combines "a privileged gaze with a new sense of brotherhood, a sensitive masculinity" (77). Arroyo points out that in *Dona Sinhá e o Filho Padre*, the narrator describes the relationship between the two male characters as a "perigosa amizade, essa desde o início com o seu toque de amor ou o seu não sei quê de sexo" [. . . dangerous friendship, from the beginning one that had a touch of love or a sexual *je ne sais quoi* (*Dona Sinhá*, in Arroyo, 69)] whereas in the sequel, *O Outro*

THE SUGAR DADDY  &#10086;  29

*Amor do Dr. Paulo*, following the death of his friend, Paulo Tavares "passara a considerá-lo, sublimando um afeto ante outro, um irmão mais moço que não tivera e sempre desejara ter. Passou a amá-lo idealmente" [started to sublimate one affection after another and ended up thinking of him like the younger brother he had always wanted. He was his ideal love (*O Outro Amor*, qt. in Arroyo, translation modified, 73)]. Arroyo concludes, "for Paulo Tavares, writing transforms itself into the search for the other part of his subjectivity, becoming the embodiment of a 'masculinized femininity' and that the ideal 'cultural fantasy' is a feminine man rather than a masculine woman" (73–74).

As suggested, I see this question in slightly different terms. What I find worth emphasizing is that even if Freyre's two novellas ultimately attempt to include or, rather, absorb the *mestizo* into the homosocial, spiritual friendship that should characterize civil society, the black man remains outside of civil society and posits a (homosexual) threat to the constitution of a (multiracial and multicultural) Brazilian subjectivity. This anxiety shows how the representation of a democratic society as a form of brotherhood underwent pointed transformations with the increasing demand for black mens' inclusion in civil society, transformations that entailed a number of contradictions that Freyre struggled to resolve. Thus, as the *mestizo* survives both the black and the white man, he retains the memory of their imagined brotherhood. But the actual racial heritage—the genetic dimension of brotherhood—is ultimately erased in the name of a culturally conceptualized "mestizo" nation. In the end, fraternal social bonds may attain a form of *spiritual* as opposed to *physical* or *biological* brotherhood; in other words, they are both de-racialized and de-sexualized.

I do realize that Freyre's "racial democracy" is not always about homosocial desire, that it is also grounded in the hyper-virility of the Portuguese man—whom he describes as the womanizer *par excellence*—and on his erotic exchanges with black women. But the sexual role of black women actually corroborates one of the situations studied by Sedgwick, in which "the routing of homosocial desire through women is clearly presented as compulsory" (*Between Men*, 49). White men and black women do not constitute a family or any type of social bond—on the contrary, the latter participate in the social construct only insofar as they mediate the contact between white and black men, sometimes as sexual objects, sometimes as wet nurses ("mãe preta" or "black mother" is synonymous with "wet nurse" in Brazilian Portuguese). Furthermore, as Vera Kutzinski suggests in *Sugar Secrets* regarding the role of the *mulata* in Cuban literature, the concept of *mestizaje* "is a trope for racial mixing without female participation" (172) which represents "the birth of a new race of *men*" (178). Kutzinski's discussion of Cuban poet Nicolas Guillén is also pertinent to Freyre's early work:

> Once the evidence of messy (that is, sexual) female participation in historical processes of racial mixing is eliminated by being made unrepresentable, *mestizaje* becomes legitimated as an exclusively male project or achievement in which interracial, heterosexual rape can be refigured as a fraternal embrace across color (and, in this case, class) lines and significantly, across a female body absented by rape. The homoerotic connotations of this embrace and the concomitant appropriation of the female reproductive function in the form of masculine creativity cannot possibly be missed. (168)

Beyond absenting the feminine, Freyre erases the participation of the black man in *mestizaje*, since he defines him as feminine and situates white men in a superior and, whatsmore, naturalized position of power. As demonstrated, though he often discusses racial contact in terms of "interpenetration," the black and the white man are always situated in asymmetrical positions with unequal power to penetrate one another (according to his own language, their contact makes one's penis grow increasingly large, while the other's becomes increasingly small). Thus, when Freyre associates the sexual indeterminateness of the Portuguese with their racial ambiguity, the resulting bisexuality does not represent a threat to their masculinity, nor does it make them less European, less white, or even less heterosexual. As paradoxical as it may seem, the bisexual and biracial nature of Freyre's notion of *mestizaje* does not disturb the hegemony of the white and heterosexual Portuguese man. Because the "flexible" Portuguese are essentially prone to assimilating external influences, they will become more and more Portuguese, or at least more Luso-Brazilian, as they incorporate African culture; furthermore, the Portuguese white boy will become more and more manly as he exchanges favors with his "black brothers." The homosexual (and yet ultimately heterosexual) model of exchange between blacks and whites is understood as a phase in the development of the Brazilian child in plantation society, as well as in the history of the *mestizo* nation. In the same way that the Greeks associated (temporary) homosexuality with a pedagogical purpose, perhaps Freyre also suggests that the ties between white men and blacks serve a civilizing purpose. In conclusion, one could say the following: (1) homosexual relations within an ethnic group are acceptable as long as they are temporary and ultimately sublimated to a "fusion of wills" (Montaigne) or a "mingling of souls" (Fiedler); (2) interracial homosocial relations are more sexually marked than those within the same ethnic or racial group; in order to become "true" friendship, they have to be de-racialized since—perhaps in the same way Montaigne perceived women—Freyre considers blacks incapable of "true" friendship; (3) the *mestizo* nation is a means for conciliating differences. It is represented by a white or whitened elite that claims to embody the nation's will—as such, it retains the principle of white male authority over subaltern groups.

Eve Sedgwick argues that "it has apparently been impossible to imagine a form of patriarchy that was not homophobic" (3), yet there is no evidence "that patriarchy structurally requires homophobia" (4). Now, Freyre's extensive work on the origins of Brazilian patriarchy may not seem homophobic, just as it may not appear racist since it celebrates the sexual and racial flexibility of the Portuguese colonizer. There is indeed an attempt to represent a gradation in the homosocial as well as racial continuum that would be hard to imagine in other patriarchal societies. Yet Freyre ultimately privileges a form of social and cultural hybridity that must always be sublimated. Just as homosexual acts may be accepted to some extent—as long as homosexuality is temporary and ultimately sublimated to spiritual friendship—blackness or the African presence must also be a transitory stage, a phase in the constitution of Brazilian subjectivity, and must therefore be transcended in the name of cultural *mestizaje* or a form of spiritual, rather than genetic, blackness.

The structures of power I identified in Freyre's representations of race and sexuality suggest a particular interpretation of Brazilian society in terms of assimilation and the effacement of difference. According to Freyre, Brazilian society is characterized by the transition from an aborted history of slavery—a relationship that corresponds to patriarchy and the benevolent father–son model—to a liberal and democratic model based on equality and fraternity. The result, for Freyre, is an original culture, facilitated by the white or *mestizo* elite that mediates between the vitality of the Indigenous and African masses, on the one hand, and the advanced intellectualism of the European, on the other:

> Between these two mystiques—Order and Liberty, of Authority and of Democracy—political life has been finding a balance, a life that has precociously proceeded beyond the master and slave regime. In truth,

the balance continues to be between traditional, profound realities: sadists and masochists, masters and slaves, doctors and the illiterate, individuals whose culture is predominantly European and others whose culture is principally African and Amerindian. This is not without certain advantages, namely, those of a duality which is not wholly harmful to our culture in the process of development, a culture which is enriched on the one hand by the spontaneity, the freshness of imagination and emotion of the most numerous and, on the other hand, by the contact, via the elites, with science, technology and the European's more advanced thought. ( *CGS*, 52)

Freyre maintains old hierarchies at the same time that he presents a model that could be viewed as democratic; he reproduces paternal paradigms of domination at the same time that he celebrates the synthesis represented by the fraternal elite. His narrative of racial democracy is constructed in the intersection of homosocial and fraternal love, on the one hand, and paternalistic and sadomasochistic eroticism, on the other. By means of what Freyre himself has defined as "bisexual writing"—not quite fictional, not quite scientific— he deploys a rhetoric of flexibility, tolerance, and ambiguity toward racial difference in ways that ultimately legitimize the univocal representation of an elite that appropriates heterogeneous, antagonistic voices in the constitution of national subjectivity.

## NOTE

1. Hermano Vianna, in a very common critical gesture of "saving Freyre from Freyre," points out that nowhere in *Casa-Grande e Senzala* does Freyre use the expression "racial democracy" ("Equilíbrio de antagonismos." *Folha de São Paulo*: Mais! São Paulo, 12 March 2000). This is true, and perhaps Freyre never employed it in any of his writings. But it is not completely by chance or solely due to misreadings that "racial democracy" became associated with his work. In *New World in the Tropics*, for example, Freyre writes about "Race Amalgamation and Ethnic and Social Democracy in Brazil" (71); he also writes that "probably in no other modern community are the problems of race relations being solved in a more democratic or Christian way than in Portuguese America (121); and that "Brazil has become prominent as a community inclined toward ethnic democracy" (167). It is also very interesting to look at the English translation by Harriet de Onís of his *Sobrados e Mocambos* (The Mansions and the Shanties). The English text was edited and modified, with Freyre's permission, and concludes with the following sentence which is not in the Portuguese version: "For Brazil is becoming more and more a racial democracy, characterized by an almost unique combination of diversity and unity" (431).

## Works Cited

Arroyo, Jossianna. "Brazilian Homoerotics: Cultural Subjectivity and Representation in the Fiction of Gilberto Freyre." In *Lusosex: Gender and Sexuality in the Portuguese-Speaking World*. Ed. Susan Quinlan and Fernando Arenas. Minneapolis and London: University of Minnesota Press, 2002.

Derrida, Jacques. *Politiques de l'amitié*. Paris: Editions Galilée, 1994.

Fiedler, Leslie. "Come Back to the Raft Ag'in, Huck Honey!" *A New Fiedler Reader*. New York: Prometheus Books, 1999. 3–12.

Freyre, Gilberto. *Casa Grande e Senzala (1933)*. Rio de Janeiro: Record, 1995 (30° ed.).

———. *Dona Sinhá e o Filho Padre*. Rio de Janeiro: Editora José Olympio, 1964. Translated as *Mother and Son, a Brazilian Tale*. Trans. Barbara Shelby. New York, Knopf, 1967.

———. The Mansions and the Shanties: The Making of Modern Brazil. Trans. and edited by Harriet de Onis. NY: Alfred Knopf, 1968.

———. *O Outro Amor do Dr. Paulo*. Rio de Janeiro: Editora José Olympio, 1977.

———. *Região e Tradição*. Rio de Janeiro: Record, 1941, 1968.

———. *Tempo Morto e Outros Tempos: Trechos de um Diário de Adolescência e Primeira Mocidade (1915–1930)*. Rio de Janeiro: Livraria José Olympio, 1975.

Kutzinski, Vera M. *Sugar's Secrets: Race and the Erotics of Cuban Nationalism*. Charlottesville and London: University Press of Virginia, 1993.

Montaigne, Michel de. *The Complete Essays of Montaigne*. Trans. Donald M. Frame. Stanford: Stanford University Press, 1989.

Sedgwick, Eve Kosofsky. *Between Men*. New York: Columbia University Press, 1985.

Vianna, Hermano, "Equilíbrio de Antagonismos." *Folha de São Paulo: Mais! São Paulo*: 12 March 2000.

# CHAPTER 3

# Writing Brazilian Culture

## *Alexandra Isfahani-Hammond*

CASA GRANDE
*senzala*
CASA PEQUENA
*sem sala*
*favela*

(BIG HOUSE
*slave quarters*
SMALL HOUSE
*no living room*
*slum)*

—*Tânia Lima*

*Unseen racially, that is, unseen as racially marked—or seen precisely as racially unmarked—whites could be everywhere.*

—*David Goldberg,* Racial Subjects, *83*

In *Casa-Grande e Senzala* (*The Plantation Manor and the Slave Barracks*, 1933),[1] Gilberto Freyre casts the intimate contact between masters and slaves as the origin for Brazilian "hybridity." Because he emphasizes the "cultural" and "atmospheric" transmission of identity, his analysis has been widely embraced as a progressive departure from eugenicist interpretations of national character.[2] What critics have failed to see is that Freyre employs these nonbiological forms of assimilation to produce a symbolically Africanized, genetically white figure as the prototype for "interracial" synthesis. This chapter shows how Freyrean hybridity proffers an ultimately exclusionary brand of assimilation that constitutes the plantation master, or the figure who emblematizes that identity, as the amalgamation of both terms of the dialectic of Brazilian culture. As Monica Kaup and Debra Rosenthal show, to utter "We are creole" is implicitly to be situated in the domain of Austin's linguistic performative (89). Accordingly, in my reading of Freyre's discussion of the writing process, I address his substitution of biological race "mixture" with mimetic *mestiçagem*, conceptualizing his text as a speech-act that produces a particular form of *mestiçagem* as it describes it.

In "From the Tropics: Cultural Subjectivity and Politics in Gilberto Freyre," Jossiana Arroyo argues that Latin American "*mestizo* projects" now popular in the humanities and social sciences need to be reappraised with attention to the exclusionary ideological currents that frequently inform them. While Arroyo investigates Freyre's "lusotropicalism" in the postwar global political context in which it was formulated, this chapter looks at Freyrean hybridization in relation to a series of postcolonial spatial dialectics—the plantation manor and the slave barracks, the metropolitan center and the colony, the anthropologist's study and the "field."

Through readings of two essays by Freyre—"Como e Porque Escrevi Casa-Grande e Senzala" (*How and Why I Wrote Casa-Grande e Senzala*, 1968) and "Reinterpretando José de Alencar" (*Reinterpreting José de Alencar*, 1962)—I look at his conceptualization of space, architecture, and atmosphere in relation to cultural—and textual— assimilation. In "Como e Porque Escrevi Casa-Grande e Senzala," Freyre lays claim to seigniorial and subaltern sites to demonstrate his authentic interpretation of Brazilian society. In "Reinterpretando José de Alencar," he attributes Alencar's assimilation of both terms of the dialectic of Brazilian culture to his "atmospheric" incorporation of non-European "values" and distinguishes him from Machado de Assis, whose mixed African-European ancestry Freyre insists disables him from inhabiting either the plantation manor or the subaltern periphery and, by extension, from articulating diverse points of view.

Both essays were written in the 1960s, known as Freyre's "conservative" period. In my readings, I make connections with *Casa-Grande e Senzala* to challenge the distinction between the "progressive, multiculturalist" Freyre of the 1930s and 1940s and the later, pro-Salazar author of *Novo Mundo nos Trópicos* (*New World in the Tropics*, 1959). I am particularly interested in taking issue with an influential study that makes a case for recuperating the "first" Freyre of the

1930s from the "reactionary" Freyre of the 1950s and 1960s: Ricardo Benzaquen de Araújo's *Guerra e Paz em Casa-Grande e Senzala e a Obra de Gilberto Freyre nos Anos 30* (*War and Peace: Casa-Grande e Senzala and the Work of Gilberto Freyre in the 30s*, 1994). Benzaquen argues that attention to Freyre's later writing has had the unfortunate effect of diminishing appreciation for *Casa-Grande e Senzala*, which he insists is a nontotalizing interpretation of the amalgamation of European and African cultures in the evolution of Brazilian society. I critique Benzaquen not only to illuminate the grounds for his specific misreading of Freyre but to draw attention to the frequently naive appraisals of "mestizo projects" in academia that read "open, ambiguous" language as evidence of egalitarianism.

## How and Why Gilberto Freyre is a Black Writer

As its title indicates, in "Como e Porque Escrevi Casa-Grande e Senzala," Freyre describes the reasons for, and circumstances under which, he composed his master work. In his description of this process, he locates himself in the interior of a "half-abandoned" house he links to the de Mello Freyre's original, plantation household and, by extension, to the site he identifies in *Casa-Grande e Senzala* as the epicenter for European/African assimilation. Located at his desk, a black servant provides Freyre with "oral information:"

> It was work that I accomplished under difficult conditions—eating once a day and living alone and isolated in a house—which still exists—on Encanamento Road, at that time the property of my brother Ulysses, where he and I, as bachelors, had lived during some years. In 1932 he was already a married man. He provided the half-abandoned house to me, and my family agreed that during the day I would be served by the old Manuel Santana, a black born in the time of slavery and for a long time a member, so to speak, of our family; and in a certain way my collaborator, through oral information, in the elaboration of *Casa-Grande e Senzala*. I learned much from this as from other Manuels, like him black and if not ex-slaves, the descendants of slaves, born in *senzalas* or in the shadow of the plantation manors, during the slavery epoch. (132)[3]

Transcribing Santana's "oral information," Freyre elaborates his text as his servant's physical presence dissolves.[4] David Goldberg's discussion of "mastering surveillance" elucidates Freyre's invocation of his servant in order to conceal him: "Recognized as black, black people at once are made visible only to be rendered invisible, to be 'dene-grified' " (87); "The prevailing logic of whiteness, then—white mythology, as Derrida puts it—is to make invisible the visible and visibly threatening" (89–90). Notwithstanding Santana's comings and goings, Freyre insists that he is "alone and isolated," the single enduring subject in their interracial exchange.

On the one hand, Freyre collapses his assimilation of black culture with the "original" transmission of black identity to whites by situating himself in a plantation-like edifice and by referring to Santana's birth as a slave. On the other, he mitigates and compliments this privilege by emphasizing that the house is "half-abandoned," that he works under "difficult conditions" and that he suffers from hunger and other physical discomforts.[5] Freyre enhances his "genuine" subaltern experience when he describes his forays in the black margins. He again invokes Brazil's original, seigniorial "Africanization" by characterizing his participation in *carnaval* and in Afro-Brazilian religious practices as a process of "resuming" previous contact:

> At the same time, I resumed, in Recife, the most intimate contacts—at bed and table, I could say—with folkloric survivals connected to the rural-patriarchal Brazilian complex: the *pastoris* and *bumbas-meu-boi*,[6] for example. I also returned to socializing with the *xangôs* after, in Rio de Janeiro, having initiated myself in the *candomblés* of Niterói and in Carnaval dances, songs and exhibitions of the then splendid laboratory for the study of African survivals in Brazilian culture, which was the Praça Onze. In Rio, I had spent entire nights in apparently merely bohemian excursions but, in truth, also study excursions, through which my knowledge of Afro-Brazilian subjects became more profound. Excursions in the company of Prudente de Morães Neto, Sérgio Buarque de Holanda, Heitor Villas-Lobos, Jaime Ovale—with the latter even through the Mangrove swamp—Dunga, Patrício, Pixinguinha. Others, in the company of Gilberto Amado. And in Bahia, the doors of Afro-Brazilian secrets opened to me, from the moment when I was introduced to the *babalorixá* Martiniano do Bonfim by his friend, the *babalorixá* Pai Adão, from Recife. (133)

Freyre's "apparently bohemian" study excursions in the public plazas and streets, together with his contact with blacks at "table and bed," produce him as an expert on "Afro-Brazilian subjects."[7] Even more importantly, the premodern connotation of "folklore," the expired original suggested by "survivals," and the transcription of

Santana's implicitly impermanent "oral information" constitute Freyre's text as the embodiment of African cultural traditions in decline. Nestor Garcia Canclini's analysis of Mexican museums' cataloguing and containment of Indigenous culture illuminates Freyre's textual incorporation of that which is "black:"

> Although they contribute to conceiving a solidary beauty above geographical and cultural differences, (the museums) also engender a uniformity that hides the social contradictions present in the birth of those works. The statues are no longer invoked, and in those museums it is impossible to know how and why they used to be invoked. It seems as if the pots had never been used to cook with, nor the masks for dancing. Everything is there to be looked at. (*Hybrid Subjects*, 120)

As with his reference to Santana as a "member, so to speak, of our family," Freyre's supernatural embodiment of blackness effaces the "genetic" assimilation evoked by his forays into the "splendid laboratory" of the public plazas and streets. At the same time, Freyre's emphasis upon his contact with the black supernatural both underscores the primacy of his textual transcription of immaterial, ahistorical blackness and sublimates his appropriation of black culture by situating it as the effect of his "initiation into *candomblé*." Like other Latin American celebrations of black culture that center on metaphysics—from santeria to vaudou—Freyre casts blackness as a chaotic force that needs to be contained.

The extent of Freyre's embodiment of that "force"—his universalized seigniorial gaze—is revealed when he declares that his narrative gives voice to all strata of Brazilian society. He first describes the task of the writer "to unfold himself into perspectives that are complementary to his own. . . . which aid him in the perception of a multiple, complex reality" (117). Emphasizing the nonunitary subjectivity that ensues from this "unfolding," Freyre refers to himself in the third person, proclaiming that "the author of *Casa-Grande e Senzala*"

> . . . . took this disintegration of personality to the truly risky, dangerous extreme of disintegrating his personality of ethnic-cultural origin and of socio-cultural formation, beyond its principally European, principally seigniorial character, to try to feel also, in his antecedents and in his own ethos, not only seigniorial but also servile; not only European but also non-European; or specifically indigenous, Moor, Jewish, black, African and, more than this: woman, boy, slave, oppressed, exploited, abused, in his **ethos** and in his **status**, by patriarchs and slave-holders. Thus

**Casa-Grande e Senzala** is a book which is multiple in its perspectives; even contradictory, in its perspectivism; vulnerable to the accusation of negrophilia. But realized in such a manner that such differences in perspective and such contradictions frequently complement each other as a corrective, in some sense, to what could be only seigniorial or attempt to conserve itself as monolithic in the personality of its author; which disintegrates in relation to certain subjects to the point where the author is more a somewhat Pirandelian composite of authors than a single author, for such is the empathy through which he attempts to perceive a single reality, contorting it and considering it from different points of view. Different and complementary: that of the man, the adult, the white but also of the child, the effeminate, the slave. Points of view, some of them perhaps never before admitted into a simultaneously profound and complex interpretation of Brazilian experience. (Freyre's bold type, 117)

Freyre declares that *Casa-Grande e Senzala* gives voice to segments of the population thus far barred from representation—to children, women, the indigenous, blacks, "effeminates" and slaves—while the subject who assimilates and articulates those voices is "principally European" and "principally seigniorial." Indeed, it is this ubiquitous identity that enables Freyre to "feel" the other's experience. With "antecedents" and "ethos," he attributes this capacity to what he claims is the originary, constitutive element of national character—the Portuguese capacity for incorporating that which is non-European.

The paradox of Freyre's seigniorial polyphony is unraveled by looking at his discussion of the ultimate colonizers in *Casa-Grande e Senzala*:

Thus, let us remember, as much the geography as the history, given its frontier situation—moveable and transitory—of Portuguese society, were made responsible for the undefined, unstable character of its inhabitants. It is worth repeating, in this regard, that this indefinition was accentuated to the point of converting the Portuguese into a unique type of *mestiço*, capable of accepting the most diverse influences, including those of a physical order, without dissolving them in an effort at synthesis, conserving them side by side, like water and oil, in that which was the first appearance of the idea of an "equilibrium of antagonisms" in this study: "Men with blond beards and dark hair. Brown-skinned men with blond hair (. . . Or rather:) mestizos with two colors of hair." (*CGS*, 218)

Freyre's "Pirandelian assimilation" of distinct perspectives is further enlightened by his stress upon slaveholders' adoption of black imperatives in which oblique pronouns are placed before rather than after verbs, such as "me dê" (*give me*) and "me diga" (*tell me*). While Freyre identifies this usage as mitigating the severity of their commands (*CGS*, 376), he at no point mentions the impact of masters' language on slaves; the absence of reverse linguistic acculturation means that whites represent all members of the national community while blacks can never speak for or about Brazil.

Whereas Benzaquen de Araújo insists that *Casa-Grande e Senzala* produces "an image of (Brazil's) extremely hybrid, syncretic and almost polyphonic society . . ." (44), attributing equal or greater importance to the impact of the *senzala* without melding the cultural exchange between the two sites into a "totalizing synthesis" (56), Freyre is clear enough: "The plantation manor, completed by the slave barracks, represents an entire economic, social, political system. . . ." (*CGS*, xiii). On the basis of the *casa-grande*'s centrality, the slaveholder's power is limitless: "The plantation manor triumphed over the church in Brazil, over its efforts to be the ruler of the land. Surpassing the Jesuit, the plantation master came to dominate the colony almost single-handedly" (*CGS*, lxvii).

## How and Why Machado Can't Write Back

In *Reinterpretando José de Alencar*, Freyre takes pains to bar Brazil's biologically conceptualized hybrid from "writing back," identifying Machado de Assis's mixed-race ancestry as excluding him from the *casa-grande* and, by extension, from the practice of writing. Though Santana enters the de Mello Freyre household as a source of information that fuels his creative endeavor, Freyre emphasizes that his servant's proper place is in the *senzala* and in the "shadow" of the plantation manor. Freyre now displaces Machado from the *casa-grande* to invalidate his critical observations of the slaveholding aristocracy. He first describes the pervasive influence of the plantation economy on Brazilian literary production, then argues that, whereas master/slave relations have had the effect of broadening the narrative range of white authors, they have had a confounding effect on writers of mixed-race origin, whose work is marked above all by the effort to efface their African descent.

Freyre declares that the impact of the "patriarchal, slavocratic complex"

> [Illuminates] the openly unsatisfied antimelanism of a Lima Barreto, on the one hand, and, on the other hand, the "arianism" which is

aristocratically superior to questions of race in its effort at discoloration—
protective, mystifying discoloration of his own skin—of a Machado: a
Machado constantly pretending to be an elite white; constantly closing
windows and closing doors against all aspects of the cruder Brazilian
landscape, of the state or city of Rio de Janeiro, in its vivid colors and
rude forms; against every grove of trees that is more indiscreetly
tropical which would remind him of his childhood on the street and on
the hill, of his condition as the son of people of color, the son of a plebeian family, the descendant of a black slave. No landscape, no color,
no trees, no sun. It is inside the house—and a house which is generally
large, a generally noble mansion—that Machado, in his novels, tries to
protect himself against the cruelty of the street and also from the cruel
view of the plebeian hills. Within the house, aristocratized in characters
of whom he is almost always the grayish eminency, to not say mulatto,
fictitiously ignobled by the mustaches and beards of the young white
master, by the spectacles of the learned gentleman who resides in a
mansion, by titles of Imperial counselor, it is thus that he defends
himself from the memory of having been born mulatto and almost in
a shanty and of having grown up as a child of the street and almost as
an urchin. (122)

Having attributed his unmitigated domain in elite and subaltern
realms to his seigniorial status, Freyre now insists that Machado's
focus on the "noble mansion" is a transgressive effort to transform
himself into an "elite white."[8] But despite his camouflage of spectacles and imperial titles, he is unable to "discolor" his skin and adopt
the perspective of the "young white master," for he is only a "grayish
eminency," a shadowy effigy of the aristocrat.

The paradox of Freyre's simultaneous celebration of miscegenation
and disavowal of mixed-race will become clearer by looking at his
treatment of race and racial mixing in *Casa-Grande e Senzala*. In this
work, Freyre claims that the Portuguese are "Afro-Europeans" due to
their absorption of black "blood" during five centuries of Moorish
domination, and insists that this "Afro-Europeanness" diminished the
conflict and coercion of Portuguese colonization. On the other hand,
he emphasizes slaveholders' nongenetic—cultural and atmospheric—
Africanization on Brazilian plantations. While in this more recent
context he effaces "blood contact," Freyre employs slaveholders'
assimilation of African culture for the same purpose, arguing that it is
the basis for their empathetic identification with their subjects as well
as for slaves' comraderie with their masters: "It was as though they
felt they were intimately their own kind on the basis of distant, merely
lightened affinities" (5). In an even more dramatic reversal of systems
of domination, Freyre argues that "the African influence boiling

beneath that of the European" produced a colonial situation in which Africa, rather than Europe, was dominant: "Europe ruled but without governing; governing first was Africa" (5).

For Freyre, there is no third term. His *mestiço* is the "Afro-European" colonizer and, chaneling that figure's legacy, the Africanized master whose coercive control is effaced by his incorporation of subalternity. Goldberg's analysis of the gaze brings further depth to Freyre's insistence upon Machado's "pretentious" depiction of the culture of the "noble mansion." He reads the dialectic of visibility and invisibility in relation to Lewis Gordon's theorization of "The sadist [as] the one who 'takes advantage of the invisible dimension of himself as seer to deny the fact of his being seen.' The sadist is a subject before whom all others are objects" (82–83). Whereas Freyre claims that Machado closes himself off to "racial questions," nothing could be less true. The problem, for Freyre, is that Machado focuses on the white aristocracy. In novels such as *Quincas Borba* (1892), *Memórias Póstumas de Brás Cubas* (1881), *Esaú e Jacó* (1904), and *Memorial de Aires* (1908), he parodies the elite's mimicry of liberal ideology in light of their acquisition of power and wealth through slavery. Machado's critique of the upper classes' duplicitous assimilation of progressive ideas is particularly stringent in *Qunicas Borba*, where he satirizes the narrator's elaboration of "humanitismo" (*humanitism*), a doctrinaire philosophy that unites evolutionist theory and liberal doctrine with social darwinism. Insisting that Machado's social analysis constitutes an endeavor to "discolor" himself and mystify his "skin," Freyre effaces his disparaging interpretation of the elite's hypocrisy by attributing that quality to Machado himself. Aggravated by Machado's assimilation of the gaze of the "young white master," Freyre insists upon his origins in the shanty and "almost as a child of the street."

## WHITE MAN IN THE TROPICS

In addition to his trespass into the seigniorial realm, Freyre identifies Machado's detachment from "nature" as further evidence of his illegitimacy. On the one hand, Freyre's claim that Machado closes himself off to the "vivid colors" and "rude forms" of the "indiscreetly tropical" landscape reflects nationalistic criticism that situates attention to nature as a standard for authentic Brazilian literature. On the other, it reflects Freyre's specific concept of the atmosphere as the medium for the transmission of identity. Whereas Benzaquen claims that Freyre uses atmospheric assimilation to demonstrate the universal capacity for adaptation, Freyre's totalizing conceptualization of "nature" is revealed when he equates Alencar with the Portuguese colonizers:

> The fact that his attitude has been, from the beginning, that of men who in these things and in these peoples discovered or perceived values to be taken advantage of and assimilated by Europeans, and not disdained or crushed as expressions of cultures wholly inferior to European ones or products of a nature which is scandalously full of sun and of vivid colors and with which the civilized, sophisticated European white would be incompatible, explains how Brazilian writers such as José de Alencar, engaged with contributing to the development of a Brazilian literature independent from academically Portuguese literature, have conserved the same spirit, the same attitude, almost the same sense of the relations between European and tropical values: the sense that one can today affirm is a characteristic of a vast, though dispersed, lusotropical culture. (139)

Freyre emphasizes that the Portuguese thrived in Brazil by incorporating indigenous and African cultural practices that were suited to life in the tropics. At the same time, he naturalizes this mode of assimilation. As in *Casa-Grande e Senzala*, where he identifies the direct impact of the climate on physiological mutations—the uniformization of "individuals of distinct genealogies" when united under the same atmospheric conditions" (*CGS*, lxii)—by qualifying those "values" as both "cultural expressions" and as the products of nature, Freyre employs natural generation to constitute a nonbiological process of hybridization. He stresses the fecundity of the Brazilian environs—so "scandalously full of sun and vivid colors"—to underscore the impact of the tropical climate on the emergence of this new "breed" of human being.

The reconciliation between European and non-Europeans "values" that displaces mixed-race—and gives rise to Alencar's distinctly Brazilian perspective[9]—echoes Freyre's conceptualization of nature and miscegenation in *Casa-Grande e Senzala*: "The miscegenation that was widely practiced here corrected the social distance that would otherwise have continued to be enormous between the plantation manor and the tropical jungle, between the plantation manor and the slave barracks" (lx). The reduced "social distance" between the plantation manor and the slave barracks describes the assimilation of seigniorial and slave cultures, while the approximation of the plantation manor to the tropical jungle "normalizes" this process; Freyre interjects the tropical atmosphere to produce the synthesis of European and African cultures as the "natural" effect of miscegenation.

Freyre displaces mixed-race authorship and establishes the symbol-ically subalternized, biologically white gaze as evidence of "authentic hybridization." This subterfuge, or trick, becomes even more glaring when he insists that, by contrast with Alencar, Machado is unable to represent interracial sex. Freyre first claims that plantation sexuality is the key to national character; as in *Casa-Grande e Senzala*, he empha-sizes its noncoercive and "social" rather than "biological" quality:

> And there is no more natural history of man—or of a society—than that of the life of its family; and this, in crude terms, is the history of its sex. The not merely biological but also the social sex of the individual. Sex more than psychoanalytically comprehended as a drive or a solicitation spread out through the entire body of this social individual: from the roots of his hair, sensitive to the scalp massage or the voluptuous click of the mulatta's hand on the young master's or young mistresses' head, on the tips of aristocratic feet, for their part quivering to the tickles provoked by the extraction, at times sweet like a sexual caress, of vermin embedded in them; and not a drive or solicitation limited to the genital organs and desirous only of coitus or copulation. (121)

Freyre's narrative of plantation sexuality emphasizes a form of noncoital—"social" rather than biological—contact that is nonethe-less procreative; the *mulata*'s "sexual caress" of the master's or mis-tress' scalp and "aristocratic feet" is the "natural" history of the Brazilian "family."

Freyre celebrates Alencar's representations of interracial couples because they corroborate his interpretation of hybridization. Like Freyre's non-child-bearing portrait of master/slave sexuality, Alencar's novels consistently efface the mixed-race offspring: it is either unborn or killed along with its non-white mother, so that the sole survivor is the nativized, acclimated European male.[10] Freyre puts this uniquely "productive" interpretation of interracial sex in place of Machado's contrastingly "sterile" treatment of the topic:

> For Machado, whoever spoke the word love—principally in a society like that of patriarchal, slavocratic Brazil, in its transition from the patriarchal family to the romantic family: one should add this nuance when referring to the rather philosophical novelist—said "complica-tion." A complication of the natural with the social the cause of which was at times the color of a man in love with a white girl; or the condition of the natural offspring of this enamored man—causes avoided by the writer who was not resigned to his condition as mulatto and almost always avid of hiding this condition. (Freyre's syntax, 124)

Since interracial love is key to the representation of Brazilian culture, Machado's "avoidance" of this topic excludes him from the Brazilian canon.[11] Even more importantly, by attributing Machado's failure to represent interracial sex to his "condition as a mulatto," Freyre dissociates the *representation* of assimilation—mimetic *mestiçagem*—from sociohistorical mixed-race identity.

Freyre's description of the context in which Machado interprets love as a "complication" gains additional depth when read in relation to his treatment of eighteenth- and nineteenth-century urbanization and industrialization in *Sobrados e Mucambos* (*The Mansions and the Shanties* 1936).[12] Discussing the substitution of the northeastern patriarchal complex with bourgeois, "romantic" or nuclear family units, Freyre identifies the *mulato* and the *bacharel* (college graduate) as the two forces that had a profound impact on Brazil as the result of urbanization and industrialization.[13] Machado's status as both a *mulato* and a distinguished intellectual explains why Freyre equates his emergence with the transition from the patriarchal to the romantic family. It also speaks to the desire to vindicate his seigniorial heritage by casting him aside both as an inauthentic Brazilian, and as an inauthentic Brazilian writer.[14]

Notwithstanding Freyre's personal investment in defending the northeastern oligarchy, there is a second, more important implication of his reference to Machado's view of love as a "complication" of the "natural" with the "social." In addition to reiterating that his biologically mixed-race ancestry confounds his effort to locate himself in any single social rank, by attributing this complication to Machado, Freyre displaces his own "complication" of the "natural" with the "social." In his work, he substitutes social, atmospheric—and, added to this, "textual"—assimilation for biological "mixture" as the source of hybridization. Ultimately, it is for this substitution of terms that Freyre has been celebrated for redeeming the African influence and for depathologizing the effects of miscegenation, despite the fact that his conceptualizations of culture and the atmosphere are markedly informed by anxiety about miscegenation and the socioeconomic ascendancy of people of African descent. As much in *Casa-Grande e Senzala* as in his later work, Freyre employs nonbiological identity formation to produce African descent as an intangible enhancement to Brazilian multiculturalism, a quality that is ultimately embodied by the northeastern plantation master.

## NOTES

1. *Casa-Grande e Senzala* was translated into English as *The Masters and the Slaves* in 1946. I employ the title's literal translation because it conveys the importance of spatial dialectics in Freyre's work.

2. *Casa-Grande e Senzala* continues to be the dominant narrative of Brazilian culture, despite the interventions of marxist critics who, beginning in the 1950s and 1960s, problematized Freyre's benign portrait of colonization and enslavement. Even many scholars who challenge aspects of Freyre's analysis corroborate the mainstream view that he redirected the discussion of Brazilian national identity from genetics to culture, identifying the perseverance of racist ideas in Brazil as evidence of an outmoded Eugenicism they insist Freyre rejected. Lilia Schwarcz claims that from the 1930s onward racist models of social analysis continued to circulate in the realm of "common sense and popular representation" *in spite* of Freyre (247). David Haberly perceives the elements of biologism in Freyre's narrative as discordant with the core of his analysis: "even Freyre could not wholly overcome the pull of the past. His obsession with African sexuality ignored his own ground-rules, confusing character and situation as completely as the arguments of most Abolitionists" (Haberly, 44).

3. This and all other translations of Freyre are mine.

4. Freyre's reference to Santana as one of many "Manuels" reflects Lewis Gordon's coneptualization of the black body as the standard for anonymity ("Existential Dynamics of Theorizing Black Invisibility," 1996, in Goldberg, 83). Gordon's invocation of Ralph Ellison in relation to sadism and race is also pertinent: he refer's to Ellison's "I am invisible, understand, simply because people refuse to see me" to show that "blackness as a project—a projection of—the white imaginary is a condition of invisibility, a mode of being unseen because unseeable" (in Goldberg, 83).

5. Freyre describes the hardship he experiences while writing *Casa-Grande e Senzala* at a number of other points in this essay: he repeats that he suffers from hunger (134), refers to his low salary (131, 132, 134) and to being harassed by the police (134). Freyre also emphasizes his impoverishment in exile in Africa and Europe following the Revolution of 1930 and immediately preceding his return to Brazil to write *Casa-Grande e Senzala* (131).

6. *Pastoris* and *bumbas-meu-boi* are popular folkloric dramatizations performed out-of-doors.

7. This duality is captured by his companions: Sérgio Buarque de Holanda, Heitor Villas-Lobos, and Gilberto Amado—iconic early twentieth-century Brazilian social scientists—and the equally iconic black samba composers, Dunga, Patricio, and Pixinguinha.

8. In addition to Lima Barreto and Machado, Freyre claims that Aluísio Azevedo attempts to "discolor" himself through writing (125). Barreto and Azevedo are nineteenth-century novelists of mixed African/European ancestry who, like Machado, satirize the ideological idiosyncrasies of the Brazilian elite. Barreto's best-known work is *O Triste Fim de Policarpo Quaresma* (1911). Azevedo's most important works are *O Cortiço* (1890) and *O Mulato* (1881).

9. In Alencar, Freyre identifies a seigniorial antecedent for his literary authority. At one point in "Reinterpretando José de Alencar," he declares that "(Alencar) was for some of us a type of distant grandfather" (133). Though Freyre does not discuss Alencar in "Como e Porque. . . .," its title is an adaptation of Alencar's autobiography, "Como e Porque Sou Romancista" (*How and Why I am a Novelist*, 1893).

10. See Alencar's *O Guaraní* (1857) and *Iracema* (1864–1865). For a discussion of these novels, see Doris Sommer, *Foundational Fictions* (1991).

11. This exclusion resonates with Silvio Romero's claim that the proof of Machado's literary failure is that he had no disciples: "The most obvious proof of the negativity of his *oeuvre* is that it had no followers, it did not nor could it have disciples; since he did not invent anything nor reproduce a single idea" (in Ventura, 98). Machado's inability to wield an impact on future writers reflects theorizations of *mestiço* sterility applied to literary productivity. Romero identifies Machado not only as part of a dying "breed" but situates his mixed-race descent as disabling him from articulating ideas that would be remembered in the future. Though Romero argues that the representation of "the races and their process of miscegenation" is key to authentically Brazilian literature, he insists that Machado, due to his mixed-race descent, is unable to depict them (*Machado de Assis. Estudo Comparativa de Literatura Brasileira*, 1897).

12. After *Casa-Grande e Senzala, Sobrados e Mocambos* is considered the most important work of Freyre's early period.

13. See Freyre's portrait of the ascension of mulattos and university graduates in *Sobrados e Mocambos*, especially 132, 168, and 368. For a discussion of the "unfortunate" ramifications of the bourgeois family structure that emerged as the result of abolition and industrialization, see 130–133 and 156.

14. For a discussion of Freyre's writing in relation to the decline of the northeast and the emergence of southeastern hegemony, see Carlos Guilherme Mota, *Ideologia da Cultura Brasileira*, 1980, 53–74.

## Works Cited

Benzaquen de Araújo, Ricardo. *Guerra e Paz em Casa-Grande e Senzala e a Obra de Gilberto Freyre nos Anos 30*. Rio de Janeiro: Editora Nova Fronteira S.A., 1994.

Freyre, Gilberto. *Casa-Grande e Senzala*. Rio de Janeiro: José Olympio, 1984.

———. "Como e Porque Esrevi Casa-Grande e Senzala." *Como e Porque Sou e Não Sou Sociólogo*. Brasília: Editora Universidade de Brasília, 1968.

———. *Novo Mundo nos Trópicos*. São Paulo: Ed. Nacional/EDUSP, 1971.

————. "Reinterpretando José de Alencar." *Vida, Forma e Cor.* Rio de Janeiro: José Olympio, 1962.

————. *Sobrados e Mucambos,* vol. 3. Rio de Janeiro: José Olympio, 1951.

Garcia Canclini, Nestor. *Hybrid Cultures: Strategies for Entering and Leaving Modernity.* Minneapolis: University of Minnesota Press, 1995.

Goldberg, David Theo. *Racial Subjects: Writing on Race in America.* New York: Routledge, 1997.

Haberly, David. "Abolitionism in Brazil: Anti-Slavery and Anti-Slave". *Luso-Brazilian Review* 9.2. Madison: University of Wisconsin Press, 1972.

Kaup, Monica and Rosenthal, Debra. J. *Mixing Race, Mixing Culture.* Austin: University of Texas Press, 2002.

Lima, Tânia. Unpublished poem, 2003.

Mota, Carlos Guilherme. *Ideologia de Cultura Brasileira.* São Paulo: Editora Atica, 1980.

Romero, Silvio. *Machado de Assis. Estudo Comparativo de Literatura Brasileira.* Rio de Janeiro: Laemmert, 1897.

Schwarcz, Lilia Moritz. *O Espetáculo das Raças: Cientistas, Instituições e Questão Racial no Brasil, 1870–1930.* São Paulo: Compahia das Letras, 1993.

Sommer, Doris. *Foundational Fictions.* Berkeley: University of California Press, 1991.

Ventura, Roberto. *Estilo Tropical.* São Paulo: Schwarcz Ltda., 1991.

# CHAPTER 4

# Authority's Shadowy Double: Thomas Jefferson and the Architecture of Illegitimacy

*Helena Holgersson-Shorter*

*Architecture is my delight, and putting up and pulling down, one of my favorite amusements.*

—*Thomas Jefferson*

The "tragic mulatto," common throughout colonial and postcolonial fiction, is a figure whose "tragedy" of perpetual displacement is ultimately subversive. As the embodiment of two theoretically irreconcilable opposites, the mulatto's presence threatens individual autonomy and identity by forcing the members of each group to recognize the familiarity of the rejected other. The mulatto often functions implicitly or explicitly as a community scapegoat, since his or her characteristic illegitimacy axiomatically affirms the legitimacy of the other members of society, her displacement ensuring that everything and everyone else is in place. Mulatto writers from different cultures and time periods such as Harriet Jacobs, Nella Larsen, and Mayotte Capécia have utilized the subversive potential of the displaced, tragic mulatto to interrogate notions of national or communal identity. This chapter looks at how the mulatto's use as agent of irony or subversion has roots in the original discourse of mastery.

To call Thomas Jefferson the father of the modern, subversively tragic mulatto is an exercise in irony on many levels. Most reasonable people now accept the fact that Jefferson fathered mixed-race children with his slave mistress, Sally Hemings. Jefferson's mulatto family, secreted within his self-designed plantation, Monticello, parallels his anxiously unstable and contradictory discourse about race and national integrity in *Notes on the State of Virginia* (1782), the only book he ever published during his lifetime.[1] I use the term "unwriting" to indicate how Jefferson the author sets out to establish the validity of a particular conclusion, but through the fraught ambivalence of his own rhetoric ultimately undermines his own argumentation. In *Notes*, unwriting occurs when Jefferson writes about race, slavery, the difference between blacks and whites, and the possibility of miscegenation. In this text, the mulatto becomes the marker of unwriting, a multidimensional manifestation of authorial anxieties. The more Jefferson tries to characterize himself as the author of *Notes on the State of Virginia* and, by extension, of the United States, the more the illegibility and illegitimacy of the mulatta threatens his own legitimacy and authority, such that his words proliferate with illegitimate meanings.

Jefferson felt that *Notes*—begun when he was governor of Virginia—had the potential to establish him as a man of letters and as a scientist, in accordance with the legacy of the man who was both his real father and the intellectual father for many members of the eighteenth-century U.S. intelligentsia. Peter Jefferson, a master surveyor, died when Thomas was fourteen. In 1751, Peter Jefferson and Joshua Fry drew up the henceforth definitive map of Virginia, which was the largest state in the Confederation and covered almost a third of the continent. Early in *Notes*, Jefferson surrenders his "authorship" of the State by deferring to his father's authority to describe the state's geography. The fact that Jefferson "frequently declared that his [father's] map was of more value than the book in which it appeared," reflects anxiety about his ability to claim his father's legacy.[2] In compensation, he tries to establish his textual authority by writing in the naturalist tradition developed by the renowned Enlightenment scientist, Georges Louis Leclerc Comte de Buffon, who was of the same generation as Jefferson's father.

In Buffon's thirty-five-volume opus, *Histoire naturelle, générale, et particulière* (1749–1788), he takes scientific facts, the *détails particulières*, and weaves them into a coherent—*general*—narrative of his own design, which then becomes "natural," or conflated with the grand design of nature. Jefferson's one-volume *Notes on the State of Virginia*, a masterful text combining geography, geology, history, ethnology, art, literature, music, law, education, and religion in Virginia, is a microcosmic satellite to Buffon's *Histoire Naturelle*.

It also maintains a running, intertextual dialogue with *Histoire Naturelle*, a dialogue that is preoccupied with defending America from Buffon's early thesis about the natural degeneracy of North and South America's indigenous species.

For Jefferson, legitimacy is inseparable from legibility. Since his discursive mastery in *Notes* parallels his rule as governor, the textual effort to discredit any prevailing concept of American degeneracy becomes intertwined with his own concerns about fulfilling a paternal legacy of mastery. To be a legitimate author is to legibly inscribe, and to have the inscribable object signify back not only the meaning given it, but also the author's authority. Jefferson presumed that his text embodied what he perceived as the infallible methodology of science. He prided himself on eschewing digressive or ambiguous language, considering those characteristics to be indicative of a lesser intellectual faculty. For instance, Jefferson praised the African-English writer Ignacius Sancho for *almost* attaining the heights of reason associated with Western European writers, but inevitably falling short due to a natural African tendency to privilege the "heart" more than the "head." His strongest criticism of Sancho's work is that he employs "sentiment" rather than "demonstration":

> . . . his [Sancho's] imagination is wild and extravagant, and escapes incessantly from every restraint of reason and taste, and, in the course of its vagaries, leaves a tract of thought as incoherent and eccentric, as is the course of a meteor through the sky. His subjects should often have led him to a process of sober reasoning; yet we find him always substituting sentiment for demonstration. (*Notes*, 140–141)

But when Jefferson presents the facts behind his theory of black inferiority, he succumbs to a bizarre and ambiguous discourse that strays from its central, intended meaning. As he strives to establish blacks' essential difference from whites along a dichotomy of black sentiment and passion versus white reason, his discourse self-consciously fights its own tendency to "substitute sentiment for demonstration." It is a struggle in which he frequently and tellingly loses control.

In *Notes*, virtually every description of black difference and inferiority to whites manifests uneasy signs of unwriting, as if the immutable border Jefferson anxiously tries to erect between the two races begins to crumble before the ink is even dry. Nowhere is this more evident than that in his passages on albinos, or blacks who erroneously appear white. It is at these moments that the unwritten figure of the mulatto haunts his text in an uncanny way, the physical embodiment of that performative border and its simultaneous undoing. It is also in these passages that the references to Buffon curiously disappear, though these are precisely the places where his debt to the renowned naturalist is strongest, since they rework the subjects Buffon covers in volume three of his *Histoire naturelle*. In Jefferson's treatment of albinos, the unstated and unwritten mulattos of *Notes*, the themes of legibility and legitimacy, difference and displacement, flow together.

## DEGENERATIVE DISCOURSE

Chapter VI, "Productions Mineral, Vegetable and Animal," is where Jefferson errs from the course charted by Buffon, leaving his "objective" authorial perch to insert himself into the text where he can confront Buffon face-to-face. But when he maneuvers to violate the boundaries erected by the masterful discourse of his "fathers," he situates himself in a position of illegitimacy, and his own discourse of mastery becomes illegible. In chapter VI, Jefferson's style begins to unwrite itself, and the crucial separation between author and the measurable, quantifiable subjects of his text begins to crumble.

In earlier volumes of *Histoire naturelle* Buffon concludes that animals in the New World are smaller, degraded versions of their European counterparts. In *Notes*, Jefferson not only invokes North American mammal fossils as evidence to the contrary, but also spends fifty pages meticulously compiling tables of weights and measurements of animals on both continents to demolish Buffon's thesis. He feels Buffon's theory of mammalian degeneracy is dangerous because of the facility of "its application to the race of whites transplanted from Europe," citing the French Abbé Raynal, who wrote, " 'One must be astonished . . . that America has not yet produced a good poet, an able mathematician, a man of genius in a single art or single science' " (*Notes*, 64). Raynal's accusation stung Jefferson, and he holds Buffon, the great metaphysical father of his text, responsible for this slight. He turns the tables on Buffon by attaching to him the stylistic markers which he will encode as signs of irrational, illegitimate discourse: "Whilst I render every tribute of honor and esteem to the celebrated zoologist . . . I must doubt whether . . . he has not cherished error also, by lending her for a moment his vivid imagination and bewitching language . . ." (*Notes*, 64). By divorcing himself and his text from its obvious progenitor, Thomas Jefferson places himself in the position of the illegitimate mulatto. Fittingly, this pivotal chapter self-consciously seizes on the mulatto as the surface upon which he can reinscribe his claim to legitimacy in a discourse ironically resplendent with "vivid imagination" and "bewitching language."

In the section of chapter VI where Jefferson describes America's indigenous animals and debates Buffon, he inserts an apparent digression on albinism among the African slaves. Though he no longer explicitly refers to *Histoire Naturelle*, this digression on the mysterious genesis and classification of "white negroes" is lifted directly from a section of the third tome of *Histoire Naturelle*, entitled "Variétés dans l'espèce humaine." In this essay, Buffon explicitly wonders about a biological connection between albinos and mulattos, then examines his facts and anecdotal information to rule out all but a superficial similarity. Jefferson's reworking of this question makes both Buffon and the comparison of albinos and mulattos conspicuous by their absences. Thus the entire albino digression becomes a shell-game of displacement, where an illegitimate or purloined textual authority struggles to validate itself through an inscription of the purloined and illegitimate whiteness of the albino/mulatto.

Whereas albinos would appear tangential, Jefferson aligns them with the loaded issue, so to speak, of a faulty New World inheritance: "I will add a short account of an anomaly of nature, taking place sometimes in the race of negroes brought from Africa, who, though black themselves, have in rare instances, white children" (*Notes*, 70). Albinism seems to be a peculiarly American problem since he does not indicate whether or not it occurs in Africa. Though Jefferson reassuringly insists that all of the albinos in question are "born of parents who had no mixture of white blood," his introduction of this subject, as well as his treatise on the dangers of mixing blackness and whiteness elsewhere in *Notes*, begs the question of under what "rare instances" black Africans in America might produce white children (*Notes*, 70). Jefferson never allows himself to discuss mulattos in any detail, yet he represents albinos as "uncommonly shrewd, quick in their apprehensions and reply" (*Notes*, 71). Blacks, on the other hand, lack the necessary mental faculties to be shrewd and quick. As implied by his seemingly unintentional praise for the "white" blacks or albinos, he later confirms that a dose of whiteness is all that is needed to bring blacks up from their base condition: "The improvement of the blacks in body and mind, in the first instance of their mixture with the whites, has been observed by everyone" (*Notes*, 141). The more Jefferson tries to establish these white Negroes as a mere anomaly of nature unrelated in any way to "true" whites, the more they begin to resemble the mulattos they are meant to replace. And the more Jefferson tries to usurp or displace Buffon's authority on the subject, the more his own text begins to fall prey to the "degeneracy" and invalidity that both authors attribute to the albinos.

What seems troubling to Jefferson about Buffon's suppressed account of albinos is their discursive resemblance to mulattos, in that they embody a strange composite of traits that he himself tries to assign to either blacks or whites. In a later chapter on "Laws," Jefferson bases his argument for white superiority over blacks on color difference. Accordingly, he must show that the albino white is not the same as the true white: "They [albinos] are of a pallid cadaverous white, untinged with red, without any coloured spots or seams" (*Notes*, 70). Racial difference is clearly fixed, he reassures us, because of its unmistakable manifestation in the visual realm of color: "Whether the black of the negro resides in the reticular membrane between the skin and scarf-skin . . . whether it proceeds from the colour of the blood, the colour of the bile, or from that of some other secretion, the difference is *fixed in nature, and is as real as if its seat and cause were better known to us*" (*Notes*, 138, my emphasis). Blackness, as a "difference" from the implicit norm of whiteness, is a difference whose causes are unknown unless we can believe that they are "fixed in nature." Inversely, the fixed quality of nature and its implied "natural" hierarchies are real only if *blackness* is "known to us," that is, "known" as the essence of *difference* from whiteness. The "cadaver" that surfaces imagistically when white color, the "universal" norm, appears on the black body, represents the death of the authority that sustains itself through the essential separation of black and white that it must anxiously and perfomatively constitute as "natural."

Jefferson's anxiety that white and black difference should validate the legitimacy of European American identity begins to merge with his anxiety about reconstituting Buffon's discourse, which he tries to control with an erasure of both the offending, spectral mulatto as well as of Buffon, the offending, spectral father. Yet when Jefferson tries to qualify the whiteness of the albinos as different from "true" whiteness, it is at precisely this moment that his text merges with Buffon's. The aforementioned passage, wherein he qualifies the albino white as "untinged with red," is quietly plagiarized verbatim from Buffon's naturalist inventory of the details of albino physiology. The essence of Jefferson's anxiety about the albino's inauthentic color is revealed in the following turn of phrase, "without any coloured spots or seams." One would expect spots or, more tellingly, seams, only if two things that were inherently and fundamentally separate were bound together. The "seamless" blending of white and black found in the albino digression begs the readers' association with another type of blending of white and black that also leaves no visible seams. Miscegenation can never produce an authentic or legitimate whiteness, but only symbolize the degradation of white superiority and the production of a body that is illegitimate by definition, and illegible in Jefferson's "natural" order.

Jefferson's conclusion of the albino digression further illustrates his strategy of rhetorically sublimating problems of legitimacy and authority. The result is an unwriting that becomes characteristic of all his discourse on race. The last case to which he refers does not involve an albino at all, but a black man who is apparently turning white:

> To these I may add the mention of a negro man within my own knowledge, born black, and of black parents; on whose chin, when a boy, a white spot appeared. This continued to increase till he became a man, by which time it had extended over his chin, lips, one cheek, the under jaw and neck on that side. It is of the Albino white, without any mixture of red, and has for several years been stationary. He is robust and healthy, and the change of colour was not accompanied with any sensible disease. ( *Notes*, 71)

Jefferson identifies for his readers a tell-tale "spot," a visual mark or seam confirming the "natural" separation of white and black. When they come together, this "spot" leaves a comforting sign of the essential difference between the two. Unlike the inexplicable whiteness of the black albino or of the mulatto, which destabilizes the fixity of the perceived "natural" order in Jefferson's *Notes*, this man's half-white face will not upset any cultural or epistemic borders. Instead, the threat to the "natural" order is submerged, undetectable. Jefferson's assurance that this change of color, from black to white, was "not accompanied with any *sensible* disease" leads one to ponder the existence of a mysterious *insensible* disease or, more appropriately, dis-ease that is capable of turning blacks into whites.

Buffon maintains that while albino males are ill-suited to reproduction, female albinos are quite fertile, producing either black or spotted children with their black male partners. It is not surprising that Buffon decides the albino male is sterile while the female is capable of producing degenerates. His excessive interest in the body of the female albino renders her as a sexualized creature. Indeed, Buffon includes a personal account of an eighteen-year-old albino woman named Geneviève whom he met and examined. He measures and dissects every part of Geneviève for the reader, and includes a neat table plotting the precise measurements of this white negresse as the viewer travels with vicarious lasciviousness down her body via the following categories: "Circonfèrence du corps au-dessus des hanches," "Circonference des hanches à la partie la plus charnue," "Hauteur depuis le talon au-dessus des hanches," "Depuis la hanche au genou" and "Du genou au talon" and "Longeur du pied."[3]

Though Buffon reminds his audience that this is not a true white woman but a white negresse, with black features and black hair, he establishes her as discursively closer to white women in a manner that eroticizes the availability of her body. While her white skin is matte and wan, it is capable of attaining that rosy blush which Jefferson defines in *Notes* as indicative of superior white beauty. Her inauthentic white becomes an authentic "reddish white" when she approaches the fire, or when "elle était remuée par la honte qu'elle avait de se faire voir nue" (Buffon, 362). The act of blushing, and her feminine modesty at the exposure of her body, associate her with the white women she almost resembles. Buffon completes Geneviève's association with miscegenation and the temptation of the mulatta when he writes, "Cette fille est très en état de produire."

By alluding to the preponderance of female albinos in Virginia, Jefferson's text discloses its rereading of Buffon's original inscription of the female albino body. *Notes* presents case histories of all the albinos known to Jefferson, relating that all but one were female. In concerning himself only with reproductive abilities, relating how many children they produced and what color they were, Jefferson wishes to shift his text's attention away from the erotically charged white/black female body. Dangerously close to embodying miscegenation, he attempts to focus on its capacity for producing servile black offspring. He concludes, "Whatever may be the cause of the disease in the skin, or in its colouring matter, which produces this change, it seems more incident to the female than male sex" (*Notes*, 71). The mulatto mistresses kept by white planters engendered illegitimate bodies who became increasingly illegible with each generation of white concubinage. Jefferson's soon-to-be mistress, Sally Hemings, embodied this legacy.[4] Her father was Jefferson's father-in-law, John Wayles, who had six children by his mulatto mistress, Elizabeth Hemings. So it is not surprising that the mulatto haunting Jefferson's albino tangent is a feminized figure who finds an easy corollary in the apparent preponderance of female albino blacks.

Jefferson is aware of the threat that these increasingly white, yet legally black bodies pose to white hegemony in the state he is so concerned with insulating from charges of degeneracy. His focus on female albinos/mulattos reflects this, and his insistence that they are fecund yet capable only of producing black children with black men can be understood as a wishful projection. While Buffon masterfully dissects Geneviève's body for scientific inscription and public exposure, his academic objectivity remains intact. The fact that Jefferson's text does not similarly touch these bodies, but attempts only to discursively contain them, demonstrates his fear of being corrupted by their powerful illegitimating potential, at the same time that his refusal to locate the genesis of his mulatto digression in Buffon's *Histoire Naturelle* places his text in a similarly illegitimate position.

## SUFFUSIONS OF "PASSION"

Discussing Virginian customs and manners in chapter XVIII, Jefferson finds himself writing about passion. In his explanation of how slavery denigrates the nation by setting an amoral example for its white children, he refers to the corruptive danger of "passion" three times in a brief chapter only a page-and-a-half long: "The whole commerce between master and slave is a perpetual exercise of the most boisterous passions"; "If a parent could find no motive either in his philanthropy or his self-love, for restraining the intemperance of passion toward his slave, it should always be a sufficient one that his child is present"; and "The parent storms, the child looks on, catches the lineaments of wrath, puts on the same airs in the circle of smaller slaves, gives a loose to his worst of passions" (*Notes*, 155). Jefferson's argument is not what one might expect: that the passionate nature of the slave corrupts the moral integrity of whites. Rather, he situates the interaction *between* the two as the culprit, as if the very *proximity* of the enslaved black subject to the white master promotes a transaction from which, semantically, the problem of passion is "produced" in his text.

Earlier in *Notes*, Jefferson has trouble establishing the slave as the locus of base passion. In his chapter on Laws, he declares that "Their [blacks'] existence appears to participate more of sensation than reflection" (*Notes*, 139). He then attempts to sustain his hypothesis that blacks and whites are different species by differentiating black procreation from white procreation. Though both races experience passion, black passion is grounded in the body and white passion in the mind: "They [blacks] are more ardent after their female: but love seems with them to be more an eager desire, than a tender delicate mixture of sentiment and sensation" (*Notes*, 139). These two sentences contradict the binary opposition between blacks and whites the entire passage seeks to establish. For if the experience of "sensation" distinguishes blacks from whites, how is it that white "love" mixes its civilized "sentiment" with precisely that "sensation"? Why are sentiment and sensation "mixing" at all in a passage ostensibly delineating difference? Joan Dayan indicates that Jefferson's original analysis was even more incriminating, that he read the unwriting in his text and thereupon revised it:

> In his manuscript the phrase originally read, "but love is with them only an eager desire, not a tender delicate excitement, not a delicious foment of the soul." He has substituted a general, more abstract definition for what was before an expression dangerously close to what he had construed as specifically black ardor.[5]

Every time Jefferson writes about passion in relation to blacks or whites, he ends up writing about mixture. In chapter XIV, when he makes a case for the "natural" separation between blacks and whites, he can't help but unwrite himself when he describes the important physical differences that function as exterior markers of interior difference: "Are not the fine mixtures of red and white, *the expressions of passion by greater or less suffusions of color in the one*, preferable to that . . . immovable veil of black which covers the emotions of the other race?" (*Notes*, 138, my emphasis). If the "mixture" of red and white qualifies "true" whiteness as opposed to the illegitimate white of the albino/mulatto, it is interesting that Jefferson illustrates the beauty of that authentic whiteness by referring to passion. "Suffusions of color" ostensibly indicates blushing, yet semantically this phrase falls between the "red and white" white race and the "immovable veil of black" of the black race. It thus produces the literal, grammatical result of the metaphorical miscegenation it suggests in spite of itself.

This illegitimate reading of Jefferson's words almost overrides their intended meaning: a passion that is located between blacks and whites, and expressed by "greater or less suffusions of color," is the miscegenating passion that engenders the mulatto. It can even be interpreted as a reference to the most feared type of miscegenation: the black man "suffusing" the white norm with greater color or, even worse, *not enough differential color*, as in the case of the threatening pied-negro boy. Even if one chose to read "suffusion of color" as the mere blush of white, feminine modesty, the image calls to mind situations wherein a blush might occur—embarrassment, anger, sexual excitement— situations not entirely unrelated to the phrase's illegitimate production of meaning in the act of miscegenation. Buffon's Geneviève blushing under the inspection of her white, male inquisitor is also recalled.

Judith Butler has a helpful model for understanding Jeffersonian unwriting. Describing the assumption of heterosexuality that constitutes "normative" individual subjectivity, she identifies the seam shared by the subject and the subject's repudiated other:

> This zone of uninhabitability will constitute the defining limit of the subject's domain; it will constitute that site of dreaded identification against which—and by virtue of which—the domain of the subject will circumscribe its own claim to autonomy and to life. In this sense, then, the subject is constituted through the force of exclusion and abjection, one which produces a constitutive outside to the subject . . . which is, after all, "inside" the subject as its own founding repudiation.[6]

By applying Butler's model to Jefferson's text, the exclusionary matrix through which the white subject circumscribes his own authority becomes clearer. This figure demarcates a zone of "unlivability" as the limit for his claim to subjectivity. Jefferson's painstakingly detailed construction of the limits, borders, and geographical constitution of the state of Virginia as the precondition for tackling the subject of race makes the demarcation of this zone both literal and graphic. Once that subject is broached, Jefferson represents blacks as abject beings who are not subjects, as "others" whose otherness sustains and produces Jefferson and, by extension, all English Americans, as legitimate and un-degenerate.

In Butler's analysis, the repudiated "other" defines not only the autonomy of the subject, but the "zone of uninhabitability." This zone is the "seam" between the two races—the mulatto—as well as the seam between Jefferson's discourse and Buffon's. Jefferson's text repeatedly erects and attempts to negate both seams. The seam is problematic because of its fecundity, because of its potential to give rise to an anxiety-inducing proliferation of illegitimate readings of white authority and superiority. Though it cannot by definition demarcate what the subject and the repudiated other have in common, perforations in the boundaries produced by unwriting reveal that the seam is also the site where both master and slave are reflected through the shared dilemma of passion.

Jefferson's painstaking *absenting* establishes a crowded liminal space that becomes the locus of the mulatto for the next two-and-a-half centuries of colonial and postcolonial literature. But it is not *Notes* alone that constructs this fraught space. Jefferson's self-designed plantation, Monticello, is the literalization of the zone of uninhabitability. Occupied by two complexly commingled families, the Jeffersons and the Hemingses, Monticello is the paradoxical place where black and white, slave and master, public reason and private passion merge seamlessly and invisibly.

## MONTICELLO'S FALSE FRONTS

Jefferson continually made improvements and additions to Monticello. One of his earliest renovations was inspired by the Hôtel de Salm, which he saw during his residence in Paris. What most inspired Jefferson about the Hôtel were its clever false fronts. In his design for Monticello, Jefferson copied this idea, making a three-storey building appear one-storey tall: second-storey windows are placed on ground level so that from the outside they seem to be extensions of the first floor windows. Skylights invisible from the ground provide light on the third floor. Jefferson saved room by designing extra-small, narrow stairways. He tucked beds away in alcoves as "space savers," and decorated bedrooms with strategically placed "light maximizing" mirrors. From the inside, multileveled Monticello looked vastly different from the one-story front it presented to the state of Virginia. The ratio of light to shadow in the house was achieved through illusion. The unified front visible from the outside served as the cover for an inside divided into different levels. It does not require a great leap of imagination to conceive that these renovations were specifically designed to reflect and contain the convoluted network of master and servant families who resided there.

Fawn Brodie writes, "Jefferson had planned an impressive central house with forty-eight-foot wings containing the service quarters. But these quarters . . . were to be covered with terraces and open outward in one direction so that they remained largely unseen. Here he followed the architect Palladio, who suggested that a house, like a man's body, should be partly hidden" (Brodie, 87–88). Just what was Monticello designed to display and to hide? The house servants of Monticello were the Hemings—Sally Hemings, along with her mother, brothers, sisters, and eventually her children, in addition to Martha Wayles Jefferson's own illegitimate, quadroon siblings whom she inherited from her father.

The home is literally that which is at the heart of the uncanny. *Heimlich* means homey, "Intimate, friendly and comfortable . . . arousing a sense of agreeable restfulness and security as in one within the four walls of his house . . . [but] *heimlich* is a word the meaning of which develops in the direction of *ambivalence*, until it finally coincides with its opposite, *unheimlich*."[7] The same friendly four walls defining the familiar space of the home also lead to a parallel space, "Concealed, kept from sight."[8] The intellectual and psychological uncertainty evoked by the presence of the "white" slave children at Monticello was noted by more than one contemporary visitor to the plantation. In 1796, Jefferson's French friend, the Comte de Volney, stayed at Monticello and wrote in his journal that "Mais je fus etonné de voir appeler noirs et traiter comme tels des enfants aussi blanc que moi" (Brodie, 287). Like the house in which they resided and were enslaved, the whiteness of these children was meant to be read as a false front. Jefferson's legitimate grandson recalled,

> [Sally Hemings] had children which resembled Mr. Jefferson so closely that it was plain that they had his blood in their veins . . . in one instance, a gentleman dining with Mr. Jefferson looked so startled as he raised his eyes from the latter to the servant behind him, that his discovery of the Resemblance was perfectly obvious to all.[9]

The simultaneity of familiarity and estrangement, discernable to all who entered Monticello, constitutes the psychological uncertainty of the uncanny wherein, according to Freud, "Everything is *unheimlich* that ought to have remained secret and hidden but has come to light" (Freud, 225).[10] Eventually, the "white" slave children of Monticello indeed came to light in a scandalous newspaper exposé by James Callender in 1802. The exposé not only smeared Jefferson's character, but played upon anxiety about the threat to national identity. Callender added sting to his accusations by employing Jefferson's own argument about racial difference and national boundaries: he used Jefferson's shadowy mulatto double not only to impugn his personal morals and to indicate the jeopardized constitution, so to speak, of the country, but also to demonstrate the mulatto double's threat to the "order" of nature.

Until very recently, the modern estate of Thomas Jefferson continued to maintain, even in the face of DNA evidence, that Jefferson's nephew, Peter Carr, was the real father of Sally Hemings's children. The Carr rumor derives from secondhand information from Jefferson's grandson and namesake, Thomas Jefferson Randolph. Randolph told Jefferson's biographer, Henry Randall, that there was a definite resemblance between the Hemings children and Jefferson, though his mother, Martha Jefferson Randolph, had told him that this was because Jefferson's nephew, Peter Carr, was their father. Randolph elaborated on how one of Sally Hemings's children looked so much like Jefferson that "at some distance or in the dusk the slave, dressed in the same way, might have been mistaken for Mr. Jefferson" (Brodie, 248). The fact that the slave boy and the patrician master resemble one another when the boy is kept in the dark or at a distance amounts to an almost Freudian slip: intended as part of an explanation as to why the boy in question is *not* Jefferson's son, it unwittingly reveals the strategies for denying Jefferson's obvious paternity. Like the strategically placed mirrors of Monticello, the slave boy's resemblance to the master can be explained as a trick of the light.

Jefferson's shadowy, mysterious, unreadable, and uncanny mulatto double haunts the limen of Monticello in the same way that his discursive predecessor haunts the textual limen of *Notes on the State of Virginia*. Whether appearing at night or standing silently behind his father/master's chair while serving dinner, he is the uncanny manifestation of Jefferson's unwriting on the subject of race.

Annette Gordon-Reed claims, "There is no reason to believe that the question of Sally Hemings could ever overshadow Jefferson's legacy to this country."[11] Yet judging from the ongoing nature of the controversy, the "issue" of Sally Hemings and Thomas Jefferson *is* his legacy to this country. The wealth of contradictions involving race, miscegenation, and representation surrounding Jefferson are part of the framework that constitute the *unheimliche heim* of Monticello, his discourse, and his actual legacy. Gordon-Reed's choice of the word "overshadow" in relation to this legacy is also appropriate. Curiously, the prolific writer, scientist, statesman, and naturalist never developed a language that would allow him to acknowledge the mixed-race individual's place either in his own household, in the State of Virginia, or in the country at large. Jefferson neither publicly acknowledged nor denied the existence of his mulatto family. His legitimate granddaughter, Ellen Randolph Coolidge, wrote in a personal letter that the notorious "yellow children" of Monticello were simply allowed to disappear when they reached adulthood: "I remember . . . four instances of this, three young men and a girl, who walked away and staid away—their whereabouts was perfectly known but they were left to themselves—for they were white enough to pass for white" (Brodie, 292).[12] One can only imagine what would have happened had these children not chosen to pass quietly away, whether they would have been subjected to reenacting the legacy of resemblance and repudiation that produced them, each motion toward the front of the house meriting a corresponding push back into the shadows.

The constant revisions of Monticello parallel its master architect's revisions of the terrain he mapped out in *Notes on the State of Virginia*, wherein he struggled to maintain blacks and whites in their separate spaces. Callender's newspaper exposé highlights the pregnant silences in *Notes*, which produced that shadowy figure capable of undoing the self-perpetuating structure of racial separateness and difference that legitimates Jefferson's authority. But perhaps more succinctly than his discourse, Monticello's false fronts, secret connecting staircases, and tricks of light and shadow provide a lasting metaphoric paradigm for mulatto representation in American culture and literature.

NOTES

1. Although Jefferson finished writing in 1782, *Notes on the State of Virginia* was published in 1784 when he arrived in Paris.
2. Thomas Jefferson, *Notes on the State of Virginia*, ed. William Peden (Chapel Hill: University of North Carolina Press, 1955), xviii. All subsequent references to this work will be cited parenthetically in the text.
3. *Oeuvres Complètes de Buffon, avec les Suites*, new edition, Tome Trosième (Paris: Chez E.L.C. Mauprivez, "Éditeur," 1836) 362. All subsequent references will be cited parenthetically in the text.
4. At the time he wrote *Notes*, Jefferson's wife Martha was still alive and her half-sister, Sally Hemings, was still a young child. Presumably, the Jefferson–Hemings affair did not begin until at least six years later.
5. Joan Dayan, *Haiti, History and the Gods* (Berkeley: University of California Press, 1998), 194.
6. Judith Butler, *Bodies That Matter: On the Discursive Limits of "Sex"* (New York: Routledge, 1993), 3.
7. Freud, *The Complete Works of Sigmund Freud*, 222 and 226; the emphasis on "ambivalence" is mine.
8. Ibid., 223.
9. This bizarre statement about resemblance and repudiation makes even less sense when one realizes that, in order for it to be true, "The Carr brothers, who lived close to Monticello, could only conceive children [with Sally Hemings] during the few months of the year when Thomas Jefferson was at Montiello. The Carr children produced under these circumstances all looked like Thomas Jefferson, and they were given the names of people who were connected to Thomas Jefferson, two of them his closest friends . . . there are no documents or statements indicating that at the time the children were being born anyone thought the Carr brothers were involved with Sally Hemings" (Gordon-Reed, *Thomas Jefferson and Sally Hemings*, 221, 223).
10. Freud, The *Complete Works of Sigmund Freud*, 225.
11. Gordon-Reed, *Thomas Jefferson and Sally Hemings*, 159.

12. Although all of Jefferson's children with Sally Hemings were named
    after members of Jefferson's family, they took the maternal last name
    of Hemings. The two oldest surviving children, Beverly and Harriet,
    were each allowed to leave Monticello at the age of twenty-one.
    They passed for white, settled in Washington D.C. and married
    white people "in good standing," according to the memoirs of
    Madison Hemings. That they were able to pass not only as white
    but also as white people of good standing suggests that they
    received some special training and education at Monticello, perhaps
    with this purpose in mind. Only Madison Hemings and some of his
    descendants chose to "remain" black, although the lack of available
    historical information about his seven daughters, beyond their birth
    records, suggests that they eventually passed for white. Eston, the
    youngest, married a racially mixed woman who was able to pass.
    After their father freed them in his will and their mother died, Eston
    and Madison moved to Chilicothe, Ohio in 1836, where they set-
    tled and were known as colored. In middle age, Eston moved his
    family out of Chilicothe to Wisconsin, where they passed for white
    and Eston changed the family's last name to Jefferson. According to
    Fawn Brodie, "The US Census of 1830 in Virginia listed him as a
    white man; the census of 1850 in Ohio listed him as a mulatto; in
    Wisconsin he was accepted again as white." Information on
    Jefferson's children is from Fawn Brodie, "Thomas Jefferson's
    Unknown Grandchildren, A Study in Historical Silences,"
    *American Heritage*, 32/33 (1976).

## Works Cited

Brodie, Fawn. *Thomas Jefferson, an Intimate History*. New York: W.W. Norton
    and Company, 1974.

Butler, Judith. *Bodies That Matter: On the Discursive Limits of "Sex."* New
    York: Routledge, 1993.

Freud, Sigmund. "The Uncanny." In *The Standard Edition of the Complete
    Psychological Works of Sigmund Freud*, vol. XVII, *An Infantile Neurosis
    and Other Works*. Ed. James Strachey. London: The Hogarth Press, 1995.

Georges Louis Leclerc, Comte de Buffon. *Oeuvres Complètes de Buffon, avec
    les Suites*. Nouvelle Édition, Tome Troisième. Paris: Chez E.L.C.
    Mauprivez, Éditeur, 1836.

Gordon-Reed, Annette. *Thomas Jefferson and Sally Hemings: An American
    Controversy*. Charlottesville: The University Press of Virginia, 1997.

Jefferson, Thomas. *Notes on the State of Virginia*. Ed. William Peden. Chapel
    Hill: University of North Carolina Press, 1955.

# CHAPTER 5

# Race, Nation, and the Symbolics of Servitude in Haitian *Noirisme*

*Valerie Kaussen*

In 1915 the U.S. military invaded Haiti citing as its excuse a particularly bloody *coup d'état*. For several weeks prior to the invasion, U.S. navy boats anchored off Haiti's coast awaited the right moment to disembark their marines and gain a foothold in the unstable nation lying too close for comfort to U.S. shores. As most historians note, the goal of the occupation was to rid the island of European influence—especially German and French—and to set up the minimum required infrastructure to assure a safe location for U.S. investment. The U.S. marines took over all customs receipts, rewrote the constitution after a rigged plebiscite to allow for foreign ownership of land and industries, and established martial law, using very undemocratic techniques in the effort to force Haiti along the road to stable "modern" nationhood.

At one time France's most fertile sugar colony, the independent nation of Haiti was founded in 1804 following a successful slave revolution and a protracted war of independence nourished by unrest surrounding the French Revolution. Throughout the nineteenth century, Haiti fiercely guarded its sovereignty in the face of escalating European, and later U.S., involvement in its economic affairs. It comes as no surprise, then, that in 1915, Haitians across the social and political spectrum perceived in the U.S. invasion and subsequent nineteen-year occupation a brutal return to Haiti's colonial past. As Jacques Roumain, celebrated novelist and founder of the Haitian communist party wrote, "the parallel between the class structure of St. Domingue and the present Republic of Haiti is quite surprising.

French colonists and American imperialists; 'affranchis' and the present day elite; slaves and the Haitian proletariat"(33).[1] After the 1804 independence, Haiti's mulatto elite, descendants of the colony's "free persons of color" or *affranchis*, indeed stepped into the shoes of the departing French colonizers, taking over government positions and becoming the new nation's landowning class. A complex race/class system operated in postcolonial Haiti succinctly summed up in the Haitian proverb, "a poor mulatto is a black man, and a rich black, a mulatto." Onto this already complex system of social hierarchization, the U.S. occupation imposed American Jim Crow style segregation and the "one-drop rule" (Plummer, 129). Haiti was returned in a sense to the degrading conditions of colonial St. Domingue where the *affranchis* or "free people of color" had legal freedom but few rights, including right of entry into white establishments.

While many a liberal Haitian described the loss of national independence as "enslavement," the impoverished black majority, as Roumain points out, were often victims of *de facto* forms of slavery. The United States reestablished the *corvée*, a type of forced labor on public works that originated in French feudalism and had not been used in Haiti since the early nineteenth century. The *corvée* militarized the labor process (chain gangs were overseen by the new U.S.-run *gendarmerie*) and incited strong public outcry. An article published in the newspaper *L'essor* intones: "the code noir, formulated in 1685 to be used in the colony of Saint-Domingue does not make sense applied to a man of the twentieth century, even if he is of African descent."[2] However, the labor practice initiated during the occupation that had the most long-term and wide-ranging effects was a system of indentured servitude, widely termed as the "slave trade" (Plummer, 111), in which poor Haitians were shipped by the thousands to U.S.-owned sugar plantations in Cuba, the Dominican Republic, and other locations in Latin America. The U.S. occupation thus initiated Haiti's all-too-familiar role in the U.S.-dominated world economy: provider of cheap labor.

An extreme nationalist movement called *noirisme*, the subject of this essay, developed in Haiti in response to the neocolonialism of the occupation. Principally led by François "Papa Doc" Duvalier and Lorimer Denis,[3] who were also its chief theoreticians, the *noiriste* movement gained momentum in Haiti toward the end of the 1930s, eventually resulting in Duvalier's election as president in 1958, the debut of one of the bloodiest chapters in the nation's history.[4] According to the *noiristes*, who also called themselves the "Griots,"

Haiti's recurrent problems, including the occupation, were the result of the suppression of the African bio-cultural element in favor of the European. Influenced both by European ethnology and theories of scientific racism à la Count Gobineau, the *noiristes* analyzed Haitian history exclusively in terms of race, the persistent conflict between the ruling mulatto elite and the black majority. The true soul of Haiti was African, and the *noiriste* goal would thus be to develop the "bio-psychological elements of the Haitian man in order to develop the material for a national doctrine" (*Oeuvres essentielles*, 114).[5] The *noiristes* pursued this goal by studying and celebrating the culture of the masses, especially the *vaudun* religion, seeing in the latter the nation's cultural "matrix" and its unique contribution to the world community, or "le concert des peuples" (*Oeuvres*, 143). *Vaudou* would furthermore function as the "supreme factor of Haitian unity" (*Oeuvres*, 205).

The *noiriste* project of cultural recovery and national renewal had its roots in *indigénisme*, a cultural nationalist movement of the 1920s that, like *noirisme*, was influenced by European anthropology and the international trend to revalorize formerly debased African cultures. Indigenist writers answered the plea of the "father" of their move-ment, Jean Price-Mars, who admonished Haiti's elite to cease its "bovaryisme collectif" and turn its gaze back to the nation's black majority for inspiration and a new national aesthetic. Members of the indigenist group, which included Jacques Roumain (later founder of the communist party), Emile Roumer, and Carl Brouard (a founding member of the Griots), came from a variety of political orientations, but their political differences tended to be downplayed throughout the occupation period to sustain the common cause of national liberation. Once the United States began to dismantle the occupation in 1930, rifts in the indigenist group emerged, with its members eventually splitting into two camps, the Marxists and the ultranation-alists, or *noiristes*.

While indigenist writers tended to be both mulatto and black, *noiriste* intellectuals generally came from the emerging black middle class of the occupation period (Nicholls, 168). Paradoxically, despite the U.S. segregation policies and blatant racism, the possibilities for social mobility for blacks improved considerably during the occupation, since for the first time in Haiti's history large numbers of blacks received postsecondary education and entered into the civil service (Schmidt, 236). Nonetheless, the U.S. occupation's "pull yourself up by the bootstraps" model of development, which allowed for mostly technical and manual education for blacks, coexisted comfortably with racist attitudes, both as the remnants of Haiti's colonial social structures and as continuing components of economic imperialism and peripheralization. Occupation officials, for example, preferred hiring light-skinned Haitians into bureaucratic posts, a policy that the various nationalist governments in the post-occupation era continued to pursue.

Neocolonialism both nourished and hampered black mobility, and the *noiristes* responded to this contradictory and bidirectional modernity by conceptualizing social mobility in terms that broke sharply with the (failed) liberal model envisioned by U.S. occupation engineers. Since the true "soul" of Haiti was African, according to the *noiristes*, blacks, not mulattos, were the nation's appropriate leaders. The black middle class alone shared the racial essence of the majority, and they alone possessed the power to represent and reflect their needs and desires. Denis and Duvalier wrote in *Le problème des classes à travers l'histoire d'Haïti* that the *noiriste* leader should function to "symbolize" and "emblematize" (15) the historical unfolding of the black masses. Indeed, the revolutionary figures Jean-Jacques Dessalines, Toussaint l'Ouverture and Mackandal had risen to power by virtue of their ability to "crystallize" the slaves' sufferings, and "incarnate" their thirst for vengeance and justice (Classe, 14). The *noiriste* notion of the leader was of course directly influenced by European fascism and by the examples of Hitler and Mussolini. *Noiriste* fascism, however, situated its principles in the local context: according to the *noiristes*, democracy was an inappropriate political model for Haiti because it did not derive from the nation's own black racial psychology (Nicholls, 172). Rather, the black nation required discipline, order, and hierarchy, a political system that would protect, as well as control, certain innate racial characteristics.

## History as Enslavement

In a number of essays written for *Les Griots: Revue scientifique et littéraire d'Haiti*, the literary and ethnographic journal they founded in 1938, Denis and Duvalier analyze Haiti's history with an emphasis upon the colonial contact period. According to the authors, this intellectual exploration would demonstrate why the nation was in a constant state of duress and why its evolution had been delayed. The occupation represented the most brutal revelation of the nation's historical derailment, and understanding its psycho-biological causes would permit a return to Haiti's own true mentality and its authentic historical mission. In an essay on the colonial period, entitled

"Question d'anthropo-sociologie: Le déterminisme racial" (1939), Denis and Duvalier quote the historian and diplomat Dantès Bellegarde who in 1925 wrote:

> "ideas, prejudices and passions [of the colonial period] have been incorporated into the character [of the Haitian people] . . . free since 1804 from French political domination, Haitians struggle to this day against the dominance of the ideas and customs under which they lived in colonial society. How many among us continue to think and act like colonizers, and how many, even more numerous, have kept the souls of slaves?" (*Oeuvres*, 121).[6]

According to Denis and Duvalier, Haiti's "problems" were partly the result of the historical legacy of colonial mastery and servitude. The *noiristes* understood colonial history as congealed in the mentality and psychology of Haiti's various racial groups. Despite its considerable limitations, it could be argued that this theory sought to account for the seemingly irrational tenacity of the past in present modes of behavior and to address the ways that historical forms are embedded in subjectivities. Postcolonial since 1804, Haiti still bore the weight of its colonial history, and the *noiristes* well understood the impossibility of wiping clean the historical slate.

In this respect, *noirisme* represents one extreme of French Caribbean discourses of decolonization that include *négritude*. The other extreme is represented by Frantz Fanon, whose *Black Skin, White Masks* calls into question *négritude* and other black identitarian cultural projects. Chapter five of *Black Skin, White Masks*, "The Fact of Blackness" is a kaleidoscopic exploration of the subjective experience of race and objectification that critiques fixed notions of raced identities, and is one of the central texts of postcolonial thought. Homi Bhabha finds in "The Fact of Blackness" a crucial illustration of the psychic structures of the postcolonial subject—hybridity, mimicry, and fetishism—that undermine unitary notions of identity, history, and subjectivity.[7] It is interesting, however, that Bhabha does not apply the same analytical tools to the conclusion of *Black Skin, White Masks*, wherein Fanon, critiquing race-based political discourses, heroically declares his freedom from history and from an ambivalent postcolonial identity. This declaration is a "revolutionary" gesture that, by repressing the past, goes against the grain of much postcolonial theory.[8]

In "By Way of Conclusion," Fanon argues that the impulse to rediscover black history addresses exclusively the "intellectual alienation" of the colonized black middle class, whose needs differ fundamentally from "the Negro who works on a sugar plantation in Le Robert" (224).[9] For Fanon, the black intellectual's excavation of his racial history becomes a means of disavowing the material realities of the present and the possibilities for revolutionary change. Explorations of the racial past thus become another kind of alienation or "enslavement," operating as counterpart to the white racist's pathology: "the Negro, however sincere, is the slave of the past . . . those Negroes and white men will be disalienated who refuse to let themselves be sealed away in the materialized Tower of the Past" (226). In contrast to a black middle class potentially alienated or "enslaved" to the historical past, Fanon identifies the black working class as paradoxically more "free": "accustomed as they are to speaking and thinking in terms of the present" (224). Writing as a Marxist, Fanon identifies the working or "enslaved" classes as the subjects of history; their position in the socioeconomic order endows them with a broader perspective on society and determines their revolutionary consciousness. Finally, Fanon declares in modernist–existentialist fashion that "I am not the slave of the Slavery that dehumanized my ancestors" (230).

Through existentialism and Marxism respectively, Fanon seeks to "liberate" both himself and the black working classes from their "enslavement" to history. This heroic declaration of freedom exemplifies what some postcolonial theorists have identified as one of the problematic gestures of decolonization: the attempt to erase the complexities of the colonial past in the interest of declaring the birth of postcolonial "new" men and societies.[10] Fanon's conclusion to *Black Skin, White Masks* interests me for two reasons. First, it provides a class critique of race-based appeals to history, which we can profitably apply to *noiriste* texts of the 1930s. Second, it demonstrates that Fanon's ultimate response to the problematic interplay between history and identity is paradoxical, since he rejects the impact of history on the formation of subjectivity and embraces the humanist ideal of individual autonomy and self-determination. By contrast, the authoritarian *noiriste* political model is based precisely upon a renunciation of this liberal (and modernist) ideal of freedom from history and tradition, as *noirisme* refused, *avant la lettre*, the existentialist–modernist faith in rupture with the past. Paradoxically, the extreme essentialism of *noirisme*, based on racialized notions of history, poses some of the same questions addressed by postcolonial theory—namely, how can we escape the colonial past when decolonization has merely recreated colonial models, stereotypes, and subjectivities? The similarities between *noiriste* and postcolonial notions of the psychic persistence of history suggest that nativist discourses, alongside nationalism and Marxism, are also part of postcolonial theory's complex genealogy. *Noirisme*, its limitations, political uses, and racism notwithstanding, should thus be historicized in terms of the contexts of its formation as well as its role in evolving discourses of history, decolonization, and postcoloniality in the French Caribbean.

While Fanon somewhat idealistically declared his freedom from history, the *noiristes* turned the problem of the persistence of the colonial master/slave model into their own solution. Recognizing the seemingly inexorable persistence of colonial psychic and social models, the *noiriste* response was sinister indeed: by condemning the black majority to a particular (biological) construction of racial history, the *noiristes* imaginatively reinforced the inherited master/slave model while carving a space for a black master class that might itself transcend enslavement to "the materialized Tower of the Past." Through scientific racism and fascist notions of the social, the *noiristes* naturalized and aestheticized history and turned mastery and slavery into unchangeable essences, the unassailable "truth" upon which their own "freedom" would be based.

According to the *noiristes*, then, who were modernist subjects indeed, history was a nightmare from which only certain unfortunates could never fully awake. In *noiriste* ethnological writings and literature, the nightmare of the enslavement to history is described in images of embodiment. History becomes a biological burden, a weight borne in the body. In "Question d'anthropo-sociologie: le déterminisme racial," Denis and Duvalier term the white genetic material introduced during the colonial period "magma," and ask how its contact with the black African could have allowed for "an elevated collective consciousness and a grand . . . spiritual ideal" (120). According to Denis and Duvalier, genetic conditioning has a material substance that limits the African race's capacity to transcend the body, to soar to ideal heights. Similarly, Maurice Casseus's poem "Colored" (1933),[11] imagines the African heritage as a solidified biological burden: the "heavy milk of atavism" and the "slow drip of ancestral blood." Images of history materialized in the body as viscous and swamp-like figure heredity as an archaic force that pulls the subject ever farther away from individualism and freedom, heredity's "enlightened" opposites.

*Noiriste* theoretical texts and *noiriste*-inspired poetry thematically reinforce this ideological procedure by representing the black race as enslaved to the very history of enslavement and by assigning to slavery the mark of the authentically Haitian. The history of slavery is turned into a myth of origins, a determining instance inscribed in the blood and coursing through veins. The middle passage to the New World is thus a repetition of the "original" story of biblical enslavement, a narrative that is prehistorical and ever-repeating. In Duvalier's own "Les Sanglots d'un exilé" the speaker recalls the long road traveled by his "ancestors of far away Africa/Boys of the wilderness/ Whose bones over centuries/of starry silence/Served to raise the pyramids."[12] Maurice Casseus, in his poem "Tambour racial" (1939) similarly writes, "it is you, poor black man and your ancient defeat that you drag along in this strange land across the harsh centuries . . . In you a bitter despair is nourished by the memory of your Nile flowing with savage waters."[13] Casseus' "Colored" (1933) also describes "shoulders collaps[ing] under the memory of the Pyramides,"[14] figuring history as the burden of racial memory. Images of biblical slavery here are not merely metaphorical, an argument that could be made about the appearance of the same trope in Harlem Renaissance or *négritude* poetry. Rather, the racial determinism of *noirisme* suggests a stronger relationship of identity and continuity between ancient history and the present. Slavery itself, in these poems, becomes typological, predetermined, and inevitable, a racial "truth" reinforced by the weight of time whose congealment becomes another signifier of the *noiriste* black subject's enslavement to the historical past.

Through the lyric "I" of these poems, however, the speaker is split, claiming modern values of individualism for himself while experiencing the pull of an "ancestral blood" that is the source of poetic inspiration. The poet's psychic split corresponds to the split between a black-identified *noiriste* elite and the black illiterate majority, and in both cases slavery functions as a means to heal and thus disavow conflict and contradiction. "Les Sanglots d'un exilé" thus represents the plight of the Haitian "race" in terms that collapse psychic alienation and physical servitude. While in the first stanza the speaker alludes to his status as a middle-class intellectual by referring to his "cold student's room," ("j'ai abandonné ma chambre froide d'étudiant"), two stanzas later he takes on the identity of a *damné*, one of Port-au-Prince's impoverished populace: "head bare, without a jacket, and belly empty" ("tête nue/Sans veste/les intestins vides") the speaker begs for "some bread, just a bit of bread" ("du pain, seulement un morceau de pain"). It quickly becomes evident, though, that physical hunger and impoverishment are metaphors for spiritual impoverishment, for the essential state of lack confronting the black man condemned to exist in the modern (white) world. In a passage that is echoed in Fanon's "The Fact of Blackness"—"while I was forgetting, forgiving, and wanting only to love, my message was flung back in my face like a slap" (116)—the speaker of "Sanglots" reaches out to the white other and is similarly met with emptiness and rejection:

> And I reached out my calloused hand slowly/With love . . . /And I kissed the void/I wanted to speak to man/But he showed me his sad grimace/I knocked in vain on all the doors/But the black of my ebony skin confounded/With the shadows of the night/And no one could see me.[15]

Psychic and physical impoverishment are both symbolized as negativity here: the speaker is invisible, indistinguishable from the night, from shadows. In Casseus's "Tambour Racial," blackness and nighttime are similarly conflated: "do not believe that down here your place is reserved in the daylight/of happiness/No, no/The day, the sun are not for you . . . /Seek your refuge in the night/The great darkness receptive to other shadows."[16] Nighttime and darkness in *noiriste* poetry refer, as Michael Dash argues, to that " 'original' night of the hold of the slave ship" (*Literature* 99), that is, to the insurmountable psychic weight of a tragic racial history. Thus, in Claude Fabry's "Le Lambi" (1937)[17] the speaker describes the "damp night" in which he still hears the "groaning" and "creaking" of the "sombre . . . slave ship" that rocks "the cradle of a race and its tragedy."[18] Through a series of metonymies, nighttime, enslavement, and the blackness of skin become condensed into a symbol signifying a collective origin in negativity. The psychic alienation of the *noiriste* elite and the misery, hunger, and physical servitude of the Haitian majority are imaginatively unified through this imagery.

The embrace of negativity is a familiar enough modernist trope. Baudelaire and Rimbaud, and the performance of the *poète maudit*, the outsider to bourgeois society, influenced black modernisms internationally and was one of the foundations of the primitivist aesthetics of *négritude*, the Harlem Renaissance, and Haitian *indigénisme*. As Dash writes, though, in *noirisme*, certain poetic themes inherited from *indigénisme* and elsewhere "degenerated into a stock set of literary postures" (98). Indeed, the idea of "blackness," here, is curiously static; it does not serve to "negate," nor subvert, nor challenge dominant epistemologies of white superiority. Not only does the *noiriste* embrace of negativity maintain racial stereotypes (the same could be said of other modernist black cultural movements), it goes much further by literalizing the *aesthetic* embrace of negativity and turning it into absence, amputation, and even death. "Mother Africa," rather than a source of cultural resistance to the West, is, like nighttime and blackness in general, categorized as part of a storehouse of images of a racial death-drive. The "womb" here is quite literally a tomb. In Casseus's "Girl" (1933)[19] and Carl Brouard's "Afrique," Africa is the cradle, not of black civilization, but of its extinction. In "Girl," "the groan of the drum of my ancestors" becomes the "profound song of a mutilated Africa" and in "Afrique," the "mysterious negro drum" is a melancholy nighttime lullaby; the "consolation of the afflicted," it puts to sleep their "immemorial suffering." Similarly, despite the memory of an African "âme héroïque et hautaine" (heroic, proud soul), the speaker of "Les Sanglots d'un exilé," unable to transcend the tragic narrative of negativity inscribed in his blood, is pulled inexorably back into the shadows of nonbeing: "I wanted desperately to attach myself/to the wings of a Dream/to grab onto a destiny . . . /But the black of my ebony skin confounds with the shadows of the night."[20] Death is the only possibility and the speaker finally resigns himself to the "silence de Nécropole."

Negation, death, and absence become symbols, here, that unify the Haitian elite and masses, and that fix history—a terrain of conflict and antagonism—into myth. In this respect, *noiriste* poetry, which elides *history* in favor of racial History as the unifying principle, clearly represents the fascism of the *noiriste* political project. Walter Benjamin wrote extensively on the literary content of the symbol and its relationship to fascist aesthetics, identifying the origins of both in the tradition of German romanticism. For Benjamin, romantic artworks create an "indissoluble" identity between signifier and signified, appearance and essence. The symbol thus unites sign and referent, creating a figure that presents itself as impervious to human history and critical dissection (Jennings, 168). In "The Work of Art in the Age of Mechanical Reproduction," Benjamin applied this notion of romantic aesthetics to an analysis of fascism: "the logical result of Fascism is the introduction of aesthetics into political life" (241), an aethetics of the "aura," in which appearance and essence, form and substance are reconciled.

This notion of a precultural and ahistorical unity is a crucial aspect of the *noiriste* aesthetic, as it is of the earliest formulations of *négritude*, the cultural and political movement developed by francophone black students, including Aimé Césaire and Léopold Sédar Senghor, in Paris of the 1930s. In his writings, Senghor viewed primordial oneness as an essential quality of the black character: "the very nature of the Negro's emotion, of his sensitivity, explains his attitude toward the object perceived with such basic intensity. It is an abandon that becomes need, an active state of communion, indeed of identification, however negligible the action—I almost said the personality—of the object. A rhythmic attitude: The adjective should be kept in mind."[21] Senghor argues that in "negro nature" and "negro art" the gap between subject/object does not exist, but rather one sees there a "communion," a unification that provides an antidote to the divisions and abstractions of the West. James Arnold has amply noted the influence on the *négritude* movement of the late German Romantic ethnologist Leo Frobenius (35–40), who argued that civilizations and peoples were the expressions, the vessels in a sense, of pre-cultural, and absolute "life forces" which he termed "païdeuma." Denis and Duvalier also leaned heavily on Frobenius's irrationalist theories of culture. In an article entitled "Psychologie ethnique et historique," they wrote, emotion or "the Païdeuma is a faculty which permits the observing subject to enter into direct communication with the subject observed. By this process, the Me does not distinguish itself from the non-Me and fusion is complete . . . the Païdeuma expresses itself on a superior plane, that of the absolute or of pure reality" (135).[22]

Benjamin's discussion of the romantic symbol applies equally to Frobenius's "païdeuma" and can help us to further analyze the *noiriste* aesthetic and its political stakes. Benjamin charges fascism with articulating a politics of the masses that evacuates the masses' demands: "Fascism sees its salvation in giving the masses not their right, but instead a chance to express themselves" (241) passively through mystified symbolic forms. Fascism thus provides the opportunity for collective expression "without affecting the property structure which the masses strive to eliminate" (241). Russell Berman puts it quite succinctly:

> Benjamin contends that fascism abandons the politics of the liberal bourgeois era, an individualist politics, while defending the bourgeois principle of private property against the collectivist desires of the "masses." (37)

Indeed, *noirisme* valorized and celebrated a racial notion of the Haitian "folk" as part of its antirational, antiliberal politics. Even as popular culture, especially *vaudou*, was given expression, the black majority would be denied a "voice" and a role in the new nation except as silent embodiments of national and racial authenticity. By writing enslavement as biologically inscribed, as a racial "truth" upon which a collective identity was founded, the *noiristes* sought the utter naturalization of colonial models of power. The *noiristes* thus envisioned a perpetuation of Haiti's colonial organization, leaving in tact the prerogatives of the "master" class as well as the marginalization and disempowerment of the majority.

For the *noiristes*, enslavement was an ideal symbol for the Haitian nation since it imaginatively contained social unrest within itself. The aestheticization of slavery served to mystify the class-based demands of the black majority, turning politics and social conflict into biological tendencies that would be appeased through literary and artistic expression such as poetry. Thus, as Laënnec Hurbon argues, "slave" revolution and unrest provided the *noiriste* elite a fictive foundation for its antiliberal nationalist politics. Hurbon explores how the notion of a black African tendency toward irrationality, spontaneity, and violence allowed the *noiristes* to view the peasant revolts that had rocked Haiti since its founding not as responses to social inequities, but as signs of the rural black masses' anarchic nature (Hurbon 92–93). According to the *noiristes*, the black personality was characterized by closeness to nature, primitivism, irrationality, savagery, ferocity, and nervousness in addition to mysticism, blacks' "marque distinctive." These racial tendencies explained why Haiti's black populace had been given to periodic outbreaks of revolution and unrest. In one article, Denis and Duvalier argue for the determining role played by African geography and meteorology in the black race's essentially unstable collective personality:

> In truth, in that "*Africa portentosa*," more than in any other region on the planet, the exterior environment has the virtue of modelling man physically and psychologically in its own image . . . at once prostrate under the overwhelming ardor of the tropical climate, at once emotional before the savage grandeur of an atmosphere charged with electricity, at once plunged into anguish by the imminence of torrential storms, the Africain of the Soudanese zone does not know the calm experienced by inhabitants of more favored climes. (195)[23]

According to the *noiristes*, the wild African environment produced a race whose psychology was based on anxiety, nervousness, and emotion. The Congolais' closeness to the "thick shadows of Equatorial Africa" ("ténèbres épaisses de l'Afrique Equatoriale") made this group especially savage and nervous: "ferocity, savagery, these are the traits that characterize a category of Congolais" (195) ("férocité, sauvagerie, voilà en réalité les traits qui caractérisent une catégorie de Congolais").

The *noiristes* justified their right to rule the country on the grounds that they alone had the power to control this restless majority. Hurbon writes that, in the *noiriste* national project, Haiti's problems would be solved, that is, social upheaval "neutralized," by finding "intellectuals able to speak for the masses, and thus keep them in a docile position" (92).[24] He points to the geopolitical context for Duvalier's nationalism when he adds that *noiriste* ideology was "a calming discourse for the local bourgeoisie as it was for the imperial metropoles" (92).

Nonetheless, the *noiriste* construction of the slave as symbol cannot totally contain the fracturing histories of class conflict, difference, and racial hybridity that characterize Haitian history and the institution of slavery. For if the racial unconscious posited in *noirisme* is the repository of the historical past including slavery, then it cannot help but give expression to the conflicting desires, histories, and demands of this heterogeneous former time. Indeed, in an article on the ethnic composition that created the Haitian people, Denis and Duvalier write that "the colonial context, [was] a veritable melting pot where multiple races blended together" and thus "you can see for yourself the battle that these different bloods and antagonistic tendencies have created in his [the Haitian man's] biology, as well as in his mentality" (187).[25] Denis and Duvalier thus acknowledge the heterogeneity and conflict of the "contact zones" created by European colonialism and the slave trade. While they view the chaotic contact of diverse "bloods" as destabilizing, as detrimental to the African Haitian soul, they nonetheless acknowledge the psyche as a force field of differences, of "tendances antagoniques." These "tendances antagoniques," internalized in the racial unconscious posited in *noirisme*, become the sites for critically dissecting the quasi-fascist aestheticization of the unequal political, cultural, and economic power relations of postcolonial Haiti.

## *Viejo*: The Racial Soul Undone

Maurice Casseus's novel *Viejo* (1935) both reproduces *noiriste* ideology and disrupts and subverts it by representing a latter-day "slave" as a symbol of Haitian racial authenticity.[26] The slave in question is a migrant canecutter, or "viejo," named Mario, who after fifteen years laboring on a U.S.-owned sugar plantation in Cuba, returns to Haiti to find his homeland under the boot of the U.S. occupation. Casseus represents Mario's labor in the cane plantations of Cuba typologically, as a repetition of the essential racial narrative of enslavement. Employing *noiriste* imagery of history as a biological burden, Casseus describes his character as "play[ing] out the destiny of a race," and carrying "upon his heart . . . the weight of a black continent with all its deserts and pyramids" (15).

But *Viejo* is also obsessed with mapping and depicting the influences that threaten the integrity of the black racial soul: the consumer culture, liberal ideologies, and cultural contact initiated by the American presence in Haiti. For Casseus, ideals of whiteness and the U.S. dollar are both vehicles carrying the insidious ideologies that assure imperial control, a form of power that works upon the subject's desires and that radically alters mentalities as well as bodies, so that those who "worship the idol of the Dollar" are transformed into a "new race" (56). This "new" or miscegenated race is the novel's figure for imperialism's new forms, its "colonization" of bodies and mentalities. The connections between miscegenation, ideology, and the market are depicted vividly in the *viejo*'s migration to Cuba. In representing modern processes of migration and contact within the context of economic and cultural imperialism, the novel cannot avoid disrupting the organic closure of the slave as symbol, repoliticizing that image, and showing that modernity itself is miscegenated, a field of tensions between classes, racial groups, and geographical regions.

In *Viejo*, then, Casseus depicts modernity as a force of degradation and desacralization, a foreign invader that pollutes the purity of nation and race. Nonetheless, in seeking to map the changing psychic, social, and geographical landscape of occupied Haiti, he cannot help but acknowledge the other side of modernity's own dialectic: the potential for self-expansion, mobility, and creativity. Indeed, the *viejo* is a figure for modernity as a process of contact, syncretism, and migration. New social types of the era, *viejos* were cosmopolitan figures created out of the conditions of U.S. imperialism in the Caribbean. *Viejo*'s Mario is thus depicted as having acquired a hybrid identity in Cuba: he sings Spanish songs on his ribbon-festoooned guitar and peppers his phrases with Spanish words. Further emphasizing his acquired real and cultural capital, Mario also has a mouthful of new metal teeth ("une mine de metal") and wears an enormous gold chain (3), making him an object of admiration for the street children who gaze at him as he passes by. Once returned to Haiti, Mario is a "new man," a modern individual who has benefited from the concentration of capital in the Caribbean under U.S. imperialism and who begins to experience a certain self-expansion, a multiplication of his possibilities. Mario emblematizes the dialectic of modernity as it has recently been described by Michael Hardt and Antonio Negri: on the one hand, he represents the creativity, dynamism, and mobility of the global "multitude;" on the other, he is subject to ideological and physical repression, including enslavement, intended to contain the threat posed by that dynamism.[27]

Casseus's depiction of unrest among the laborers on the cane plantation likewise expresses this modern dialectic. In Cuba, responding to low wages, Mario organizes a labor strike in commemoration of the Haitian Revolution and its black nationalist leader, Jean-Jacques Dessalines: "it was me who told the Haitians of the 'central' that we should go on strike on January 2, in memory of Dessalines, and organize a revolution in the 'Centrals' of Camaguey because of the salaries" (27–28).[28] On the one hand, this depiction of revolution on the cane plantation clearly reinforces the *noiriste* attempt to fix and contain history: the Haitian Revolution is "resurrected" as a typological event, a symbol of the archaic Haitian nation, and an emblem of the ever-repeating narrative of white/black conflict in Haiti. But on the other hand, the transnational and multicultural character of the Cuban sugarcane plantation, with its American managers and workers from Cuba and Haiti, disrupts this symbolization of servitude as the basis of racial and national identity, and the scene of labor struggle in Cuba insists as much on the modernity as the archaicism of black revolution. Furthermore, the scene's climax takes place in the modern space of the sugar-processing factory; strewn with the detritus of industrial production, it provides the *mise-en-scène* for the articulation of Mario's demands in the language of Third International communism. A performance of Haiti's national epic, the scene's signification nonetheless exceeds this nationalism. Through juxtaposition and implication, Casseus associates the Haitian Revolution with an *alternative* Caribbean history of modernity that includes labor resistance, with a mass movement produced by the intercultural contacts and dialogues that derive from labor migration and capital flows.

But *Viejo*'s exploration of black revolution is perhaps most important for its attempts to understand the *aftermath* of revolt, and provide a window into the anxieties that produce the *noiriste* notion of the closed *âme raciale*. In the novel, a struggle to the death between Mario and his American manager paradoxically initiates a crisis, a shattering of the certitude of Mario's role as emblem of the black racial soul. In a kind of primal scene that refuses a simplistic understanding of how the past impacts the present, Mario spends a dark night of anguish wrestling with his conscience over the death of the white manager. Now an outlaw ["I was exactly twenty-four years old and I had just killed a man" (29)], Mario is pursued by authorities who want to hang him. At the same time, he feverishly lives through his existential crisis, splitting his own consciousness into accused, jury, and judge: "his own judge, Mario condemned himself. Two Mario's were there: the one that wandered through the cool Havana night, devoured by fever, and the other that travelled through the maze of his own conscience" (30).[29] A thematization of the *noiriste* notion of racial miscegenation as a psychological battle, these passages depict the formation of a "mongrel" unconscious, a split subjectivity. By representing the psyche as the product of the individual's experience of history, *Viejo* reveals the disavowed reality of conflict and difference implicit in the *noiriste* racial soul and tentatively attempts a more psychoanalytic rendering of the relationship between past and present.

Yet what these passages in *Viejo* also demonstrate is that *noiriste* anxiety about miscegenation and interracial social contact is partly addressed to a different form of servitude: ideology, in the sense of social control and social regulation. Ideology, here, must include the Enlightenment discourses of freedom and rights that partly inspired the Haitian Revolution and Independence (as well as Third International communism). In the passages that follow the manager's killing, Casseus meditates upon the kinds of "freedom" that modernity truly offers. Mario, the liberated "slave," is indeed a "new man." But rather than occasioning real freedom, his rebirth signifies his entry into a different form of subjection. Having internalized the Law and accepted his transgression, Mario now carries his prison within: "Mario of yesterday, a prisoner of Mario today, newly born" ["Mario d'hier prisonnier du Mario d'aujourd'hui, nouvellement né" (29)]. Modernity as the "iron-cage" of rationalism internalized by self-regulating subjects is metaphorized in the passage where Mario internalizes the ghost of the former "Master:" "within him there were burning coals, because he remembered having killed. Alongside his own heart there now lived another that a hand had stabbed; on his tongue was the taste of blood" (29).[30] Mario's rebirth as a "new man" finally disrupts the progressive revolutionary narrative that would imagine the end of slavery. Casseus switches his concern from "slave" emancipation to postcolonial subjectivity. But the recognition that the other is within, that is hybridity, becomes not a source of subversion or resistance, but a new means of control. Emancipation initiates the colonization of consciousness by rational and functional systems of thought, so many new forms of enslavement. Mario is like Hegel's modern European men who "remain enslaved even as they carry their Lord inside themselves."[31] This extended meditation upon freedom and modernity is once again contained by the novel's narrative voice, now turned authoritarian, as it insists anew upon Mario's role in the novel: "something must have happened, because the man rediscovered the ferment of hate and revolt that someone had breathed into his bones in a long ago age . . . No. No remorse, but one hundred percent hate. Mario you must struggle one hundred percent for the defense of your crucified race!" (32).[32]

In opening up the *noiriste âme racial*, Casseus is confronted with the postcolonial problematic of identity and history, problems to which he can find no new solutions. What do we do with the persistence of the colonial past in the present? How do we imagine liberation from the past, when the notion of liberation is forever tainted by European modernity and its exclusions, regulations, and hierarchies? Like *noirisme* and contemporary postcolonial theory—unexpected bedfellows indeed—Casseus regards with suspicion the attempt to escape history when colonial psychic structures persist not only in the unconscious of the colonizer, but also in that of the formerly colonized. Postcolonial theories find a solution in the processes of hybridity and mimicry, signs of the complex dispersion of power through subjects and locations for resistant and subversive politics. But writing in the maelstrom of transformations initiated by the neocolonialist U.S. occupation of Haiti, Casseus, and the *noiristes* in general, mistrust such solutions, associating racial and cultural hybridity with new forms of servitude that operate on the level of the psyche as well as the body. *Viejo* redirects the notion of ideology as regulatory mechanism to questions of power in the postcolonial context and thereby reveals one of the contexts for the production of *noiriste* fascism and its notion of a closed racial soul. The novel reveals the ways in which modern imperialism's contradictory politics are internalized, albeit incompletely, by its subjects, often becoming the foundation for their own visions of national liberation.

## Notes

1. Translation is mine.
2. Quoted in Gaillard, *Les Blancs*, 100. Translation is mine. "Le code noir, formulé en 1685, à l'usage de la colonie de Saint-Domingue, cela ne se comprend pas, [appliqué à] un homme du XXème siècle, même s'il est descendant d'Africain."

3. A third member, Louis Diaquoi, is also credited with the founding of the *noiriste* group, who also called themselves the "Griots." Diaquoi died in 1932.

4. Both Nicholls and Gaillard (*La Destinée de Carl Brouard*) write that the intellectuals associated with the founding of *noirisme* (Denis, Duvalier, and Diaquoi) began meeting as early as the 1920s, with Diaquoi announcing the formation of the group called the "Griots" in 1932.

5. From "L'Essential de la doctrine des Griots" reprinted in *Oeuvres essentielles*. All references to *Oeuvres essentielles* refer to this edition. All translations of Denis and Duvalier are mine. Original French appears in the endnotes. "les éléments bio-psychologiques de l'homme haïtien afin d'en tirer la matière d'une doctrine nationale."

6. "ces idées, ces préjugés et ces passions [of the colonial period] s'é-taient incorporés à leur substance morale: . . . libres depuis 1804 de la domination politique de la France, les Haïtiens luttent jusquà présent contre la domination des idées et des moeurs sur lesquelles a vécu la société coloniale. Combien parmi nous pensent et agissent comme des colons et combien plus nombreux sont ceux qui ont gardé des âmes d'esclaves."

7. See, e.g., Introduction to *Black Skin, White Masks*, and *The Location of Culture*, chapter 2.

8. Similarly, J. Michael Dash reads Fanon's *The Wretched of the Earth* as promoting an idealistic notion of history cleansed of its complex-ities. See, *The Other America*.

9. All references to Fanon refer to Charles Lam Markmann's transla-tion, *Black Skin, White Masks*.

10. See, e.g., Ahmad, *In Theory*.

11. In *Entre les lignes*. Translations of Casseus's poems are my own. Exceptions noted.

12. In *Oeuvres*, 240–241. "Ancêtres de la lointaine Afrique/Les gars de la grande brousse/Ceux-là dont les ossements pendant "des siècles/De silence étoilé"/Ont servi à ériger les pyramides."

13. Saint-Louis and Maurice Alcibiade Lubin, 402–403. "Tambour Racial" was first published in the journal *Les Griots* in 1939. "C'est toi, pauvre nègre et ta déchéance millénaire,/que tu traînes sur cette terre inconnue/A travers des siècles d'amertume./ . . . /Il y a , en toi, un âpre désespoir que peuple le souvenir/de ton Nil aux eaux barbares."

14. *Entre les lignes*, 41-43.

15. "Et je leur ai tendu ma main calleuse, lentement/Avec amour. . ./Et j'ai embrassé le vide/J'ai voulu parler aux hommes/Ils m'ont mon-tré leur rictus douloureux/J'ai frappé en vain à toutes les portes/Mais le noir de ma peau d'ébène se confondit /Avec les ombres de la nuit/Et l'on ne me vit même pas."

16. Quoted and translated by Dash, *Literature and Ideology*, 99.

17. Reprinted in Saint-Louis, 423.
18. Quoted and translated by Dash, *Literature and Ideology*, 99. "La nuit moite sent . . . gémir/la membrane craquant et sombre du négrier/du négrier qui, sur la mer lasse, berce l'infortune d'une race."
19. *Entre les lignes*, 38-40.
20. "j'ai voulu désespérément m'accrocher/ Aux ailes du Rêve/De me river à une destinée . . . /Mais le noir de ma peu d'ébène se confondit/Avec les ombres de la nuit."
21. "Ce que l'homme noir apporte," quoted in Fanon, *Black Skin, White Masks*, 205. "La nature même de l'émotion, de la sensibilité du nègre, d'autre part, explique l'attitude de celui-ci devant l'object perçu avec une telle violence essentielle. C'est un abandon qui devient besoin, attitude active de communication, voire d'identification, pour peu que soit forte l'action, j'allais dire la personnalité de l'objet."
22. "le Païdeuma, autre faculté qui permet, lui, au sujet observateur et pensant d'entrer en communication directe avec le sujet observé. Par ce processus le moi ne se distingue pas du non-moi, la fusion est complète . . . le Païdeuma, s'exerce sur un plan supérieur, celui de l'absolu ou de la réalité pure."
23. "En vérité, dans cette 'Africa portentosa,' plus qu'en nulle autre région de la planète, le milieu extérieur a la vertu de modeler à son image, l'homme physique et psychologique . . . tantôt prostré sous l'ardeur accablante d'un climat tropical, tantôt ému devant la sauvage grandeur d'une atmosphère chargé d'électricité ou encore plongé dans l'angoisse par la perspective imminente des inondations torrentielles, l'africain de la zone soudaine ne saurait présenter cette quiétude des habitants des contrées favorisées" (195).
24. "il n'y a qu'à trouver les intellectuels aptes à parler pour les masses, à les tenir dans une position de docilité, à neutraliser tout bouleversement social."
25. "dans le cadre colonial, véritable creuset où de multiples variétés de races se sont fondues pour le générer, vous vous représenterez la bataille que ces sangs diverses et ces tendances antagoniques se livrent dans sa biologie, autant que dans le champ de sa conscience morale."
26. See my article, "Hereditary Antagonism: Race and Nation in Maurice Casseus's *Viejo*," in *French Civilization and Its Discontents: Nationalism, Colonialism, Race* ed. Stovall and Van Den Abbeele. New York: Lexington Books, 2003.
27. See Mardi and Negri, *Empire*.
28. "c'est moi qui avais dit aux haïtiens de la 'central' qu'il fallait faire la grève le 2 Janvier en souvenir de Dessalines, et organiser une révolution dans les 'Centrals' de Camaguey à cause des salaires."
29. "Son propre juge, Mario se condamne. Deux Mario sont là: celui qui erre par une nuit fraîche de Havane, dévoré de fièvre, et l'autre qui chemine par les longves dédales de la conscience."

30. "Il y a en lui une braise ardente, car l'homme se souvient d'avoir tué. Un autre coeur est logé à côté de son coeur, qu'une main poignarda, et sur sa langue est le goût du sang."
31. Quoted in Gilroy, *The Black Atlantic*, 50.
32. "quelque chose a dû se produire, car l'homme a retrouvé ce ferment de haine et de révolte qu'on souffla dans ses os à une époque partie . . . Non, non, pas de remords, mais la haine cent pour cent, Mario, la lutte cent pour cent pour la défense de ta race crucifiée!" (32).

## Works Cited

Ahmad, A. *In Theory: Classes, Nations, Literatures.* Oxford: Oxford University Press, 1992.

Arnold, James. *Modernism and Négritude: The Poetry and Poetics of Aimé Césaire.* Cambridge: Harvard Press, 1981.

Barman, Russell. *Modern Culture and Critical Theory: Art, Politics, and the Legacy of the Frankfurt School.* Madison: University of Wisconsin Press, 1989.

Benjamin, Walter. "The Work of Art in the Age of Mechanical Reproduction." In *Illuminations.* Trans. Harry Zohn. New York: Schocken Books, 1969. 217–251.

Bhabha, Homi. Introduction. *Black Skin, White Masks.* By Frantz Fanon. London: Pluto Press, 1986.

———. *The Location of Culture.* London: Routledge, 1994.

Casseus, Maurice. *Entre les lignes.* Port-au-Prince: Editions "La Presse," 1933.

———. *Viejo.* Port-au-Prince: Editions "La Presse," 1935.

Dash, Michael. *Literature and Ideology in Haiti, 1915–1961.* London: Macmillian, 1981.

———. *The Other America. Caribbean Literature in a New World Context.* Richmond: University Press of Virginia, 1998.

Denis, Lorimer and Francois Duvalier. *Le Problème des classes à travers l'histoire d'Haiti.* 2nd ed. Port-au-Prince: Au Service de la Jeunesse, 1958.

Duvalier, Francois. *Oeuvres essentielles,* 3rd edition. Port-au-Prince: Presses Nationales d'Haïtti, 1968.

Fanon, Frantz. *Black Skin, White Masks.* Trans. Charles Lam Markham. New York: Grove Weidenfeld, 1967.

Gaillard, Roger. *Les Blancs débarquent.* Port-au-Prince: Presses Nationales: impr. Le Natal, 1973.

———. *La Destinée de Carl Brouard.* Port-au-Prince: H. Deschamps. 1984.

Gilroy, Paul. *The Black Atlantic: Modernity and Double Consciousness.* Cambridge: Harvard University Press, 1993.

Hardt, Michael and Antonio Negri. *Empire.* Cambridge: Harvard University Press, 2000.

Hurbon, Laënnec. *Culture et dictature en Haïtti: L'imaginaire sous contrôle.* Paris: L'harmattan, 1970.

Jennings, Michael. *Dialectical Images: Walter Benjamin's Theory of Literary Criticism*. Ithaca: Cornell University Press, 1987.

Nicholls, David. *From Dessalines to Duvalier: Race, Colour and National Independence in Haitti*. New Brunswick: Rutgers University Press, 1979.

Plummer, Brenda Gayle. *Haiti and the United States: The Psychological Moment*. Athens and London: The University of Georgia Press, 1992.

Roumain, Jacques. *Analyse schématique*. 1934. Port-au-Prince: Editions Idées Nouvelles, Idées Prolétariennes, 1981.

Saint-Louis, Carlos and Maurice Alcibiade Lubin. *Panorama de la poésie haïtienne*. Port-au-Prince: H. Deschamps, 1950.

Schmidt, Hans. *The United States Occupation of Haiti, 1915–1934*. New Brunswick: Rutgers University Press, 1971.

Senghor, Leopold. Sédar "Ce que l'homme noir apporte." *L'Homme de couleur*. Paris: Librairie Plon, 1939.

# CHAPTER 6

# Fanon as "Metrocolonial" Flaneur in the Caribbean Post-Plantation/ Algerian Colonial City[1]

*Nalini Natarajan*

*. . . how did [novels] "read" cities? By what narrative mechanisms did they make them legible and turn urban noise into information?*
   —*Franco Moretti*, Atlas of the European Novel (79)

*. . . the Plantation continued to exist [in] . . . the region's cities*
   —*Antonio Benitez-Rojo*, The Repeating Island (66)

This essay investigates conceptualizations of race, gender, and consciousness that came into play with the abolition of slavery and post-plantation urban development. Through a reading of Frantz Fanon's *Black Skin, White Masks* (1967) and *The Wretched of the Earth* (1963), I consider his discussion of urban space as symptomatic of the ideological dialogue between two streams in critical theory, post-slavery and postcolonial studies. By reading Fanon's texts with reference to the specific city spaces he observes—Fort de France, Martinique in *Black Skin, White Masks* and Algiers, Algeria in *The Wretched of the Earth*—we can enter into a fruitful discussion of how the coexistence of class, gender, and race in Fanon's urban spaces compares with the rest of the Caribbean and other parts of the French Empire. While Fanon theorizes the Algerian colonial city as a space that encompasses Arab peasant and middle classes—homogenized in his discourse to the single term, "native," that segregates and distinguishes him from the

French settler—in the Martinican case, he focuses only on the "native" Creole urban middle classes. He ignores the urban poor, despite the fact that living spaces occupied by slaves and ex-slaves in many Caribbean cities were thoroughly mixed with those of the colonizing and Creole residents (Higman, 96–97). Such an omission has important implications for Fanon's insertion in the field of "Black Atlantic" studies, where the Afro-Caribbean urban classes have been key.

I want to contextualize this study of the architectural dimensions of Fanon's discourse within two frames. The first relates to colonial and postcolonial cities' built environments and public spaces, which are permeated by imperial, nationalist, and post-plantation ideology and history. Theorists of urban space have posited the colonial city as a contact zone, beginning with the imperial idea that it is a peripheral locale to which "core" metropolitan culture is carried (King, 13) and whose resulting hybridity enables as well as threatens metropolitan control. The emerging middle classes and the rural poor move into postcolonial cities and share urban spaces in culturally specific ways. As Antonio Benitez-Rojo notes (66), in post-slavery contexts, the plantation gives way to the city; urban space is usually marked by the movement of large sectors of hitherto enslaved populations to the city. I address the ways that the post-slavery Caribbean city emerges as both repressive post-plantation locale and utopian space of possibility.

I also want to contextualize this essay is relation to the internal psychopathology of colonized subjectivities. Within this second frame, I read the heterogeneous space of the modern colonial city as "uncanny"—a space of unfamiliarity. Though all modern cities embody what Anthony Vidler terms "personal and aesthetic estrangement" (ix–x), colonial alienation suggests a specific set of socio-psychoanalytic variations.

To unite the two frames I have outlined—the "writing" of the-colonial built environment and urban colonial psychic alienation—I posit Fanon as a colonial *flaneur*, partaking of *metropole* and colony and disturbed by this "metro-colonial" experience (Valente, 632–633). Though revolutionary, Fanon is like other colonial travelers who, in Antoinette Burton's terms, explore "spatial and cultural contingencies" (Burton, 156) as colonial subjects. He has characteristics of the traditional *flaneur*, moving precariously between different worlds, attempting to privatize social space (Benjamin, 10) and infiltrating colonial reality with his metropolitan perspective.

Because Fanon is the preeminent psychoanalyst of the effects of colonization, my emphasis on external reality in his work goes against the grain of Fanon studies. His theories of colonial subject formation (highlighted by Henry Louis Gates, Jr.), the mutual interpenetration of Europe and its colonies (highlighted by Edward Said), and ambivalence and Manichean delirium (highlighted by Homi Bhabha) address internal consciousness. I concentrate, instead, on the outer world of built environments in Fanon as a bridge between post-plantation and settler ideologies and their effects on consciousness. Such attention to external architecture and city spaces will bring a new perspective to the constituent elements of Fanon's status as a "global theorist" (Gates)—his theories of subject formation, the West's construction of its others and "ambivalence."

## CARIBBEAN CITIES: BENITEZ-ROJO ON FROUDE

The Caribbean city has been the subject of much literary and cultural representation as well as theoretical discussion. I provide an overview of such discussion by referring to Antonio Benitez-Rojo's interrogation of J.A. Froude's classic colonial depictions of Caribbean cities. Froude's comparison of Kingston and Havana—"Kingston is the best of our West Indian towns and Kingston has not one fine building in it. Havana is a city of palaces, a city of streets and plazas . . . "—leads Benitez-Rojo to a discussion of the effects of asymmetrical plantation experiences in the Dutch, English, French, and Spanish regions (35). He compares Spanish settlement colonies (62) with the exploitation colonies of England, France, and Holland, and concludes that the Plantation city was "scarcely more than an urban precinct dominated by sugar warehouses, commercial offices . . . . the governor's mansions, the fort, the docks and the slave shacks . . . ."(63).

For Benitez-Rojo, a civic order predates the plantation in the Spanish towns:

> . . . . cities such as Kingston, Bridgetown, Georgetown, Cayenne, Fort de France, Paramaibo had been built in fact as plantation ports; they answered the requirements of societies, where, on average, nine out of every ten inhabitants had been slaves at one time, and this fact made it superfluous . . . . to think of improving levels of urbanization, institutionalization, education, public services and recreation. Although slavery had already disappeared when Froude visited the Caribbean, the Plantation continued to exist, and the region's cities still showed the marks of their recent slaveholding past. (66)

Viewed from the perspective of Fanon's Fort de France and Algiers, which represent both colonial and exploitative types of settlements within the same Imperial power, Benitez-Rojo's distinction becomes more complex. His seeming condescension toward the "plantation ports"—where former slave societies were deemed unworthy of civic improvement—is problematized by his reference to the fictional city, San Andres, wherein he reveals his conception of the "solar," a patio attached "to a colonial house with illegally tapped electricity and no running water." Though "backward" by European standards, the lack of material resources goes hand in hand with the creative "creolité" of the Caribbean city: ". . . it is a variegated social cell, a dense melting pot that cooks together several religions and beliefs, new words and dance steps, unforeseen dishes and musical styles . . . .the yard or solar is a result of the plantation" (211).

Benitez-Rojo is clear that this space is not to be confused with postindustrial urban slums; this is a premodern space, engendered by the plantation. It is an anti-plantation, characterized predominantly by "negroes" but by mixed ethnicities as well. These people are not "lumpen" but self-employed people, with knowledge of local crafts such as mask-making; they are not located in the business centers or rich residential areas of the city, but in the old town. The plantation histories of such Caribbean cities can lead to a creative wealth, a focal opposition to forces of hegemonic global capital. Benitez-Rojo associates the post-plantation Hispanic Caribbean city with pre-plantation European grandeur, Creole enterprise, and Afro-Caribbean creativity. The combination of these elements in the "solar" could be read as sublimating class struggle to a conflict-free, postmodern space.

On the other hand, Benitez-Rojo implicitly reads the port—the dockside or the "duelle"—as a violent space where "the memory of the skin" or "inherited racial prejudice" (211) prompts the perpetuation of plantation attitudes. Racial newcomers who threaten the status quo (such as the "Spanish Man" of Fanny Buitrago's novel) are exterminated by the island's "traditional spirits" who continued "to practice discrimination between Negroes and whites" (206). In both Benitez-Rojo's ethnological/cultural/discursive account and Gordon Lewis's political account, Caribbean cities are connected to a subversive discourse of piracy, carnival, and other eruptions of "lower-class" modes of life into the high European feudalism of Plantation Ideology.

Literary representations of the Caribbean city are also characterized by such dual vision. Novel after contemporary Caribbean novel registers the misery of the urban slum—in *Minty Alley* (C.L.R. James, 1936); *Black Shack Alley* (Joseph Zobel, 1980); *Miguel Street* (V.S. Naipaul, 1959)—while noting how that misery is mitigated by heterogeneous urban experience. For V.S. Naipaul, "A stranger could drive through Miguel Street and just say 'slum!' because he could see no more. But we, who lived there, saw our street as a world, where everybody was quite different from everybody else" (56). The city offered more social exposure, greater freedom of movement, and economic options to free and enslaved Africans. Enslaved Africans also developed new skills whose marketability they discovered, including the possibility of exchanging their labor for freedom. The city could be a pan-American, Harlem-like nexus of creativity where a renaissance of poetry and music flourished (Everson, 5). Examples of representations of this dynamic space are the "barrack yard" fiction of Trinidad, a genre not without its ideological problems (Sander; Everson, 12), as well as novels that depict the democracy and openness of the city, including an emphasis upon carnival.

In contrast to these theoretical and literary representations of the laboring classes, in his account of Fort de France in *Black Skin, White Masks*, Fanon refers only once to the lower classes, to servants speaking Creole (20). I explore this eloquent absence in the pages that follow.

## THE URBAN INFRASTRUCTURE IN FANON

Fanon's usefulness for postcolonial theories of race, desire, and violence has had the effect of blunting the complexity and specificity of the multiple locations from which his theories are formulated. The combination of generality and emphasis, metaphor and lived experience in Fanon's writings suggests his universal relevance for theorizing decolonization. Fanon's writings take on a trans-geographical and trans-historical validity that serve the interests of postcolonial theory (Macey, 26–27). The following extract from Homi Bhabha is paradigmatic. For Bhabha, it is

> One of the original and disturbing qualities of *Black Skin, White Masks* that it rarely historicizes the colonial experience. There is no master narrative that provides a background of social and historical facts against which emerge the problems of the individual or collective psyche. (in Macey, 26–27)

Fanon's text moves between abstract, general categories such as native and settler, colonizer and colonized and refers to Antilleans, Arabs, Blacks, and Africans in confusing ways. Though a decade separated the writing of *Black Skin, White Masks* and *The Wretched of the Earth*, the tautological or repetitive persistence of the Manichean binary model persists (McClintock, 362). Notwithstanding Bhabha's claim, the master signifiers can be read as the specific built environments and consequent human phenomenology of the two cities in which Fanon lived, Fort de France and Algiers. Fanon was an observer—a highly politicized *flaneur*—of the two cities, their citizens, and their distinct approaches to colonialism.

## MACEY AND FANON: FANON'S GROWTH AND THE CITY

David Macey's recent biography, *Frantz Fanon* (2000) provides insight into the physical contexts that informed Fanon's theories of consciousness. Macey employs a variety of sources—newspapers, journals, interviews—to evaluate Fanon's spatial references and to juxtapose his personal evolution with the topography of Fort de France.

> Fanon became Algerian, or, to be more accurate, recreated and defined himself as Algerian but he could eradicate neither the influence of the time and place of his birth nor the circumstances in which he grew up. His relationship with the island where he was born was complex and tormented but he was born on and of that island. In some respects, Fanon remained Martinican to his death. (31)

Macey describes Martinique's identity crisis: though located in the Caribbean, the island is culturally conceived as part of France, with its capital in Paris (33). "Overseas Departments" such as Martinique live a half-life, for "even as it is insisted that Martinique is French, it is hinted that it is not quite in France" (34). The island's shadowy relationship to France means that its usage of French is odd, its people oversensitive, its history, except that of the French minority, nonexistent (39). At the same time, in school atlases and geography lessons, Martinique is an exotic paradise that is confusingly indistinct from the rest of the Caribbean: "The beach and the palm tree could be in any of these places [Martinique, Reunion, Guadeloupe, Tahiti]" (35). That Martinique could have a distinct non-European culture produced by the transplanted slaves and "coolies" (Indian indentured labor from Pondicherry who replaced the Africans after emancipation), is never suggested. But if Martinique is French, it is a generic paradise island, a "department" as well as "French, but not quite" (31–37).

Macey's description of the built environment of Fort de France—the product of the plantation economy, with its minority *beke* population, its "shadism," unemployment, and the island's subservient, dependent relation to France—suggests that the colonization of Martinique is informed by a dichotomy between revolutionary and colonial France. This dichotomy is embodied by the two statues that mark Fort de France's topography: of the abolitionist, Victor Shoelcher, and Napoleon's empress, Josephine, a Martinican Creole by birth. Republican and abolitionist traditions, celebrations of France's egalitarianism, are reflected in street names such as Rue de la Liberte, Rue Lamartine, and the Rue Victor Hugo. Macey points to the removal of Josephine's statue's head and to grafitti on Schoelcher's statue as moments of urban resistance that pay clandestine tribute to libertarian France in this essentially colonial city, a space that stands in striking contrast to Riviere-Pilote, a Martinican city with a much more radical history (Macey, 10).

> The streets of the little southern town of Riviere-Pilote tell a different story from those of Fort de France. A plaque in the Rue du Marronage records the history of the runaway slaves or maroons who launched armed attacks on the white plantations. . . . Nearby, a plaque in the Rue des Insurrections Antiesclavagistes records the history of two centuries of slave rebellions . . . .(of) revolt in le Carbet . . . . St. Pierre . . . . Le Lorrain . . . . (11)

Macey notes that Fanon, though born and raised in Fort de France, felt uncomfortable there and preferred the more radical ambience of Riviere-Pilote. But Fanon neither mentions the Riviere-Pilote insurrections, nor considers the urban areas that housed the descendants of slaves, the Martinican counterpart of Benitez-Rojo's "solar," or the Anglophone islands' "barrack yard." He does not mark the city as a site of resistance, but only of mimicry. Rather than explore this omission, Macey reads Fanon's obliviousness to the evidence of slave revolts in city spaces as "a telling indictment of the history he was taught at school" (43).

In the passages from *Black Skin, White Masks* that follow, Fanon's descriptions of Fort de France center on the small bourgeoisie living in an area delimited by "Canal Levassoir to the west, the park town known as the Savanne to the East, the boulevard de LeLevee to the North and the sea to the South" (Macey, 52). He begins his account of colonial pathology with a hypothesis on space. Colonialism introduces a gradation whereby colonial province, colonial capital, metropolitan province, and metropolitan capital are arranged in succeeding orders of importance. This spatial hierarchy is transmitted to the island's inhabitants, who travel to the metropolis to imbibe a "transferred value." The following quotations from *Black Skin, White Masks* details this hierarchy: "There is the city, there is the country. There is the capital, there is the province" (19); Just as the Lyonnais "boasts" of the beauty of Paris, the "Process repeats itself with the man of Martinique" (19). But even Fort de France

> . . . .is truly flat, stranded. Lying there naked to the sun, that flat, sprawling city, stumbling over its own common sense, winded by its load of endlessly repeated crosses, pettish at its destiny, voiceless, thwarted in every direction, incapable of feeding on the juices of its soil, blocked, cut off, confined, divorced from fauna and flora. (Aime Cesaire, *Cahiers d'un retour au pays natal*, 1956, 30, in Fanon, *BSWM*, 21)

In Martinique, the European city is typically set on a hill; it dominates the landscape and represents the point of reference the colonized seek for validation. Fanon describes acceptance into the high society of Diddier, the preserve of the richest people in Martinique, "with its dazzling houses," as "Hegel's subjective certainty made flesh" (44).

The layered quality of the built environment reflects and is reflected in a consciousness that is mimetic, imitative. Unlike the simple binary opposition wherein one term excludes the other, here the other mimics the one. The non-French inhabitants—the Martinique "whiteys," in Mayotte Capecia's words, "who are not too pure racially but who are often very rich—it is understood that one is white above a certain level"—covet Diddier. For men, entry into this space signifies "becoming" white, while for women it signifies marrying "white." The dialectic of being and having characterizes Antillean society. Identity is conferred by wealth, and the supreme symbol of that wealth is a house in Diddier.

In the following quotations from *Black Skin, White Masks*, Fanon situates travel to the urban centers of the metropolis as a further means for determining power:

> . . . .the most eloquent form of ambivalence is adopted toward them [the returning Martinicans] by the native, the one who had never crawled out of his hole, the *bitaco*. (19)
>
> . . . .the man who is leaving next week for France [meeting his friend in Savanne] creates round himself a magic circle in which the words Paris, Marseille, Sorbonne and Pigalle become the keys to a vault. (23)

> At the Savannah, where the young men of Fort de France spend their
> leisure, the sides of the square are . . . bounded by worm-eaten
> tamarind trees, one end marked by a huge war memorial, the other by
> the central Hotel . . . . (24)

Like Didier, the Savanne is another colonially marked urban location,
a site of homosocial bonding where Martinican men newly returned
from France establish their superiority.

Where, in this narrative, are the slums of Martinique, the loci
of post-slavery populations fleeing the plantation? It will be useful
to recall that the French Caribbean followed a unique historical
trajectory:

> The plantation system outlived the abolition of slavery, which was not
> accompanied by any land reform. Writing in 1843, the great liberal
> Alexis de Tocqueville had argued that: "Whilst the Negroes have the
> right to become free, it is undeniable that the colonials have the right
> not to be ruined by the Negroes' freedom." (Macey, 42)

Only a small minority of those "liberated" after emancipation even
managed to move to the town, to occupy the "black shacks" of
Zobel's novel. Fort de France was disease-ridden. In 1952, the year
*Black Skin, White Masks* was published, it was composed of "shacks of
rusty corrugated iron, barefoot children dressed in brownish rags, worn-
out adults dragging their deformed legs in the dust . . ." (Macey, 53).

The absence of the post-slavery subaltern in Fanon's oeuvre as well
as in Macey's biography leaves us with an image of petit bourgeois,
imitative Fort de France, a city in the throes of a postcolonial identity
crisis. This image contrasts strikingly with Fanon's representation of
colonialism in *The Wretched of the Earth*. Whereas the colonial space
of Martinique becomes a site for extinguishing native "otherness,"
Fanon emphasizes the conflictive, polarized relationship between
settler and native in Algiers.

Though Fanon conflates Antillean, Arab, and African as shifting
signifiers for the colonized native, the civic geography of *The
Wretched of the Earth* is very different from that of *Black Skin, White
Masks*. Anger replaces assimilationist subservience, for the colonized
Algerian "is patiently waiting until the settler is off his guard to fly at
him" (*Wretched*, 53). Whereas the inhabitants of Fort de France
desire to whiten themselves by acquiring wealth, the Algiers native
envies what the settler has but does not wish to become him.

Much of *The Wretched of the Earth* was composed following Fanon's observations of Algerians in Lyons, whom Macey describes as follows:

> In the 1920s and 1930s the deteriorating economy of Algeria forced many peasants—the majority of them from Kabylia—to migrate and find work in Lyons' factories. Others had simply stayed on after being demobilized during the First World War. In the early 1930s the Algerian community in Lyon was estimated to be 2,200. Most were single men, living ten or twelve to a room in the slums of the Rue Moncey and the Guillotiere' quarter . . . According to a 1923 police report, "the Rue Moncey was a nest of filth, a centre of anti-hygiene, a threat to public order and a social danger." (121)

Fanon's descriptions of Algiers appear to refer more directly to Lyons' slums than to the towns of the Maghreb: "The town belonging to the colonized people, or at least the native town, the Negro village, the medina, the reservation, is a place of ill-fame, peopled by men of evil repute. It is a town of niggers and dirty Arabs" (39).

One of the primary differences between the colonial topography of Fort de France and Algiers is the accessibility of the metropolis. While in *The Wretched of the Earth*, the native's world is circumscribed, surrounded, the principle for colonial dominance in Martinique is the possibility of "being" through "having." The French in Algeria made no attempt to develop a class of middlemen or "native elites" (Young, 277). Thus, Algiers' Arab community was located entirely within the Casbah, the fortress of the old city, an "Arab town embedded in a European city" (Macey, 471). Fanon's Manichean, compartmentalized depictions of Algiers are not imagined projections; they are literal representations of architectural styles that do not apply to Martinique.

Fanon does not appear to be aware of Arab architectural preferences and how they were manipulated by the colonialists. The following remarks of the French architect, Marechal Lyautey, reveal how these preferences were evoked to justify urban planning strategies in the colony:

> The embryos of indigenously sparked modern districts were appropriated by the foreign ruling class . . . . (in Abu-Lughod, "Moroccan Cities," 81)

> The natural tendency of Europeans upon entering a foreign place is to pre-empt the center which causes both the European and the native to suffer (in Abu-Lughod, 95).

> Large streets, boulevards, tall facades for stores and homes, installation of water and electricity are necessary . . . . making the customary way of life impossible. (in Abu-Lughod, 93–94).

You know how jealous the Muslim is of the integrity of his private life, you are familiar with the narrow streets, the facades without opening behind which hides the whole of life, the terraces upon which the life of the family spreads out and which therefore must remain sheltered from indiscreet looks. But the European house is the death of the terrace . . . . Little by little, the European city chases the native out, but without thereby achieving the conditions indispensable to our modern life. (in Abu-Lughod, 95)

Lyautey argues that the colonial city should be built outside, enclosing the native city. Notwithstanding his professed concern for preserving Arab culture, his motives are clearly exploitative; ethnic separation and the containment of insurrection and disease motivate "surrounding" the Arab town. David Theo Goldberg has analyzed the effects of this colonial policy of "granting" autonomy to the Arab quarters. For Goldberg, the European city enclosed the native city, controlling the Arab's entry or escape from its borders. Such colonial planning meant that the colonized were controlled and patrolled from within the rulers' orbit, and that they were invisible both to themselves and to the colonizer, while the colonizer reserved for himself the prerogative of the urban gaze of surveillance (188).

Fanon refers to this reality of Algerian urban architecture, mediated by his recent experience of Algerian ghettos in Paris:

> The colonial world is a world divided into compartments . . . The colonial world is a world cut in two. The dividing line, the frontiers, are shown by barracks and police stations. (38)

> The zone where the natives live is not complimentary to the zone inhabited by the settlers . . . The settler's town is a strongly built town, all made of stone and steel. It is a brightly lit town; the streets are covered with asphalt, and the garbage can swallow all the leavings. (39)

Despite the inconsistency of Fanon's references—and particularly his conflation of Arabs, Africans, and Antilleans—his analytic models are quite specific. In his descriptions of Algeria, the binarisms of colonialism are embodied in the spatial colonization of the city.

While the built environment of Fort de France is reflected in the mimetic consciousness of its inhabitants, the polarized layout of Algiers leads to resentment and envy among the bourgeoisie and a more radical, confrontational stirring among the peasantry. We thus encounter two versions of Manicheanism, both produced and reinforced by urban architecture: imitation, or what Glissant has called "the mimetic drive" in Martinique, and " revolutionary separatism" in Algiers.

Fanon's discourse on language in *Black Skin, White Masks,* and on radio in *The Wretched of the Earth,* further illustrates this difference between the mimetic and the revolutionary. For Fanon, the Martinican's adoption of French illustrates his desire to mimic, to be white, whereas the Algerian people reject the radio as an instrument of colonial values, as "part of the eternal round of Western petty bourgeois ownership" (1959, 149). His discussion of the veil and the *foulard* (head scarf) underscores this contrast. Whereas Fanon reads the Algerian woman's veil as a self-chosen barrier that allows her to control her space—"Removed and reassumed again and again, the veil has been manipulated, transformed into a technique of camou-flage, into a means of struggle" (*Studies in a Dying Colonialism,* 1959, 61)—the Martinican woman's *foulard* signals her capitulation. For Fanon, it is the item she waves to her departing French lover, an item whose colonialist symbolism is traced in Lafcadio Hearn's euphoric, exoticized depictions of *les Porteuses* (the women porters carrying wares to and from different areas of Martinique): ". . . . the pretty foulards—Azure and yellow in checkerings; orange and crimson in stripes; rose and scarlet in plaidings; and bronze tints . . ." (113).

Though Fanon's transregional perspective could be misread as conflating cultures, he does provide architecturally specific accounts of distinct French colonial models. Unfortunately, his disgust with Martinican mimeticism, especially by contrast with Algeria's revolu-tionary separatism, does not lead him to evaluate the different forms of oppression in both contexts, the richness of post-slavery cultures or the post-slavery urban migrations that give Caribbean cities their unique Creole character. Likewise, Fanon perceives Algeria simply as the wretched of the French metropolis—Lyons or Paris—without insight into Arabs' ordering of space.

### NOTE

1. I wish to thank my research assistant, Susan Meltzer, for her assis-tance with this project. I am particularly grateful to her for bringing my attention to David Macey's biography of Fanon and for her help in summarizing it.

### WORKS CITED

Abu-Lughod, Janet. "Moroccan Cities: Apartheid and the Serendipity of Conservation." *African Themes.* Abu-Lughod, I, ed. Evanston: University of Illinois Press, 1975.

Benitez-Rojo, Antonio. *The Repeating Island: The Caribbean and the Postmodern Perspective*. Durham: Duke University Press, 1992.

Benjamin, Walter. *The Arcades Project*. New York: Belknap, 1999.

Burton, Antoinette. *At the Heart of Empire: Indians and the Colonial Encounter in Late Victorian Britain*. Berkeley: University of California Press, 1998.

Cesaire, Aime. *Cahiers d'un retour au pays natal*. Paris: Presence Africaine, 1956.

De Baleine, Philippe. *Les Dansevses de la France*. Paris: Plon, 1979.

Everson, Sally. "From Plantation to Urban Yard: Caribbean Cities as Nexus of Past and Future." Unpublished paper, 2002.

Fanon, Frantz. *Studies in a Dying Colonialism*. New York: Monthly Review Press, 1959.

———. *The Wretched of the Earth*. New York: Grove Press, 1963.

———. *Black Skin, White Masks*. New York: Grove Press, 1967.

Gates, Jr., Henry Louis. "Critical Fanonism." *Critical Inquiry* 17 (Spring 1991): 457–470.

Goldberg, David Theo. "Invisibility and Super/Vision: Fanon on Race,Veils and Discourses of Resistance." *Fanon: A Critical Reader*. Ed. Lewis Gordon. Oxford: Blackwell, 1996.

Lyautey, Marechal. Speech delivered at the University of the Annales, Paris, December 1926, 445–446.

McClintock, Anne. *Imperial Leather: Race, Gender and Sexuality in the Colonial Contest*. New York and London: Columbia University Press, 1975.

Handley, George. *Postslavery Literatures in the Americas*. Charlottesville: University Press of Virginia, 2000.

Hearn, Lafcadio. "Les Porteuses." *Two Years in the French West Indies*. New York: Harper and Brothers, 1923.

Higman, B.W. *Slave Populations of the British Caribbean 1807–1834*. Barbados, Jamaica and Trinidad: University of West Indies Press, 1995.

King, Anthony. *Urbanism, Colonialism and the World Economy: Cultural and Spatial Foundations of the World Urban System*. London and New York: Routledge, 1990.

Lewis, Gordon. *Main Currents in Caribbean Thought: The Historical Evolution of Caribbean Society in its Caribbean Aspects, 1492–1900*. Baltimore and London: Johns Hopkins University Press, 1983.

Macey, David, *Frantz Fanon*. London: Picador, 2000.

Moretti, Franco. *Atlas of the European Novel*. New York: Columbia University Press, 1998.

Natarajan, Nalini. "Woman and the Modern City in Rohinton Mistry's *A Fine Balance*." *Woman and Indian Modernity: Readings of Colonial and Postcolonial Novels*. New Orleans: University Press of the South, 2002.

Sander, Reinhard. *The Trinidad Awakening: West Indian Literature of the Nineteen Thirties*. New York: Greenwood Press, 1998.

Valente, Joseph. " 'Double Born:' Bram Stoker and the Metrocolonial Gothic." *Modern Fiction Studies* 46.3 (Fall, 2000): 632–645.

Verges, Françoise. "Creole Skin, Black Mask: Fanon and Disavowal." *Critical Inquiry* 23.3 (Spring, 1997).

Vidler, Anthony. *The Architectural Uncanny: Essays in the Modern Unhomely.* Cambridge: MIT Press, 1996.

Young, Robert. *Postcolonialism: An Historical Introduction.* Oxford: Blackwell, 2001.

# CHAPTER 7

# From the Tropics: Cultural Subjectivity and Politics in Gilberto Freyre*

*Jossianna Arroyo*

> *It is like entering another world. The coarse grass, milky-green in colour, barely conceals the white, pink or ochre-coloured sand produced by the surface breaking up the sandstone floor. The vegetation consists of only a few gnarled and scattered trees with thick bark, glossy leaves and thorns [. . .] But it only has to rain for a few days and this desert-like savannah is transformed into a garden [. . .] In a European landscape, you find clearly defined shapes bathed in diffused light. Here what we consider as the traditional roles of the sky and the earth are reversed.*
>
> —*Claude Lévi-Strauss,* Tristes Tropiques

> *And Brazil is so different even from Spanish America as to ask for special treatment in any anthropological or sociological study. So specifically Brazilian in its way of being both "Latin" and "American" that some have gone so far as to suggest that its mystery reminds one of China or Russia: it could even be described as a tropical China.*
>
> —*Gilberto Freyre,* New World in the Tropics

## "FROM THE TROPICS"

What are the main contradictions of thinking from the tropics? For the Brazilian sociologist-ethnographer Gilberto Freyre—as for many postcolonial thinkers from Latin America and the Caribbean—this question speaks to larger issues of subjectivity and representation. It addresses social confrontations and power shifts between self and other; at the same time, it alludes to the quest for a modern episteme that both represents and articulates the sociopolitical realities of the individual Latin American and Caribbean nations.

The two quotations above reflect the principal references one encounters in definitions of the tropics. In the first, the French anthropologist Lévi-Strauss concentrates on natural beauty and, in a confessional and melancholic tone, describes the view of the northern Amazon from the higher plains as "another world" in which a garden is created after a few days of rain, and "the sky and the earth are reversed." In the second, the *tristes* and magical *trópiques* are transformed into a locus for epistemology, Brazil. Gilberto Freyre articulates what it means for Brazil to be both Latin and American—with a difference. In a typically Freyrian punchline, he compares Brazil with Russia, a continent with diverse languages and ethnicities and, finally, describes it as a "tropical China."

For the European ethnographer-observer, the tropics remain the site of romantic nature, a garden of liminality, excess, and subjective loss. For Freyre, whose insider/outsider perspective as a native ethnographer confronts the reality of thinking from Latin America, to understand Brazil means to define a new episteme. This episteme, or border gnosis, to use Walter Mignolo's term, contradictorily conceptualizes Brazilian diversity in relation to two Eastern superpowers, Russia and China. Writing during the Cold War, Freyre makes these two principal threats to Europe and the United States the models for Brazil. For Freyre, both Russia and China have managed to unite diverse ethnicities into a single nation, creating advanced political cultures with little influence from the West.

If the tropics, as Nancy Leys Stepan argues, are about understanding the main contradictions of Western modernity, dispossession, and colonial expansion, they are also about representation and processes of knowledge. They are not outside the global spaces of coloniality created by the West but are located, rather, in sites that inscribe, dialogue, and subvert Western views of modernity. Slavery shaped modernity in the tropics. Therefore, thinking from the tropics is also about tropical and colonized peoples who have been stereotyped as carriers of rare tropical illnesses, as racially degenerate, effeminate, and oversexed. Writers and thinkers from the tropics have located themselves as the others inside the West, a particular subjective position in which culture becomes the panacea (and origin) of knowledge.

Recent criticism in the fields of Latin American, Caribbean, and Latino/(a) Studies has looked at modernity as a discursive paradigm for redefining political, economic, and cultural representations in the globalized world. For Román de la Campa, this reading is a necessary praxis endowed with the "ability to deconstruct identitarian longings without erasing the theoretical readings of the modern period" (x). Identity constructs and the location of new forms of agency—social, political, and economic—are central to these approaches. In the globalized world, the specificity of "talking from" a particular place—and about subjects and concepts that travel—opens up a critical frame for understanding theories that, though related to national or local problems, are inscribed in translocal positions.

Gilberto Freyre was a scholarly rather than an economic migrant, first as a student and Visiting Professor in the United States, later as a *cigano de beca* (fellowship gypsy). These experiences had an important impact on his scholarship, including his canonical works, *Casa Grande e Senzala* (1933), *Sobrados e Mucambos* (1936), and *Ordem e Progresso* (1940). As a delegate for Pernambuco after 1945, Freyre's participation in conferences throughout Latin America provided a point of departure for his theories of the shared cultural and common knowledge of Latin and Hispanic cultures, whose political force he believed would be able to overcome the advance of imperialism.

In this essay, I analyze Gilberto Freyre's definition of *tropicalismo* and discuss its importance for dialogues about subjectivity and transnational identities in the age of globalization. Conceived in the late 1940s and disseminated in lectures in Portugal and Latin America during the 1950s and 1960s, Freyre's *tropicalismo*—a theory based on the originality of the tropical man—has been widely criticized, principally because of its apology for Portuguese colonialism in India and Africa and for Oliveira Salazar's regime in Portugal. At the same time, like Fernando Ortiz's transculturation, *tropicalismo* has gained popularity in fields such as anthropology, history, and contemporary cultural studies. One of the main problems with the re-appropriation of theoretical frameworks like transculturation and *tropicalismo* in U.S. academia is that the local arguments, particularly those related to race and racisms, are lost. Some of these readings nonetheless contain important political insight for understanding contemporary debates about identity and politics. I address the racial discourses that have been erased in recent readings of *tropicalismo*, and analyze it as a science "from the tropics" that emerges at a particular historical moment in Brazilian and Portuguese history. I also discuss Freyre's *tropicalismo* in relation to his conceptualizations of *lusotropicalismo* and *hispanotropicalismo* as well as in the context of his political position in Brazil in the late 1950s and 1960s. I close my argument by looking at current uses of terms such as "tropicalization" in Latino Studies, and the possibility of an epistemics "from the tropics" for understanding social, political, and literary transformations in the globalized world.

## IN THE NAME OF BRAZILIAN CULTURE AND POLITICS: *Tropicalismo* EXPORTED

Freyre's *tropicalismo* is a composite of local and European ideas. It is informed by Pernambucan views of masculinity, eugenics, and civilization, particularly Agamenon Magalhães's conceptualization of *nordestino* identity in works such as *O Nordeste Brasileiro* (1921). For Magalhães, influenced by Euclides da Cunha' conundrum of land, climate, and man, northeastern Brazil contained "a solução mais vital dos problemas nacionais" [*the most vital solution for national problems* (81)]. Freyre brings a psychological and more "modern" perspective to Magalhães's claim that different types of northeastern men, such as the *sertanejo* (backlander) and the *matuto* (backwoods-man), will overcome racial degeneracy through education and the mastery of nature. His work is also marked by nineteenth-century European conceptualizations of the tropics, such as Alexander Humdbolt's, and by the turn-of-the-century substitution of evolutionary theories for romantic beauty in discussions of nature. It is at this point that terms such as "tropicalism," "tropical disease," "tropical degeneracy," and "tropicalismo" emerge, all with negative connotations. For Freyre,

> "Tropicalismo" uso-se e abuso-se em Europa como expressão pejorativa ou depreciativa. A eloquencia era tropicalismo. "Tropicalismo" a má literatura. "Tropicalismo" a música, a pintura, a arquitectura menos conformadas com as idéias francesas de medida e os patrões Victorianos de colorido.
>
> (*"Tropicalism" was widely used in Europe as a pejorative, dismissive expression. Tropicalism was eloquence. Bad literature was "tropicalism." "Tropicalism" described the music, painting and architecture that least conformed to French standards or to the Victorian gauge for that which was colorful,* 15).

Though Freyre intended to contest these negative views, his definition of tropicalism emerged at a moment of political crisis.

Freyre's *New World in the Tropics* (1959) is an expanded edition of *Brazil: An Interpretation* (1945), a series of Patten Foundation

Lectures delivered at the University of Indiana in 1944–1945. The expanded edition in English, published in 1959, reflects a marked change in tone and perspective. Published in the year of the triumphant Cuban Revolution and four years after Getúlio Vargas's suicide left Brazil in a political and military crisis, it is evidently more grim and insecure. The world was witnessing the decolonization and independence of India, Africa, and the Caribbean, and the constant manipulation and intervention of two political enemies, Russia and the United States. For Freyre, Brazil's future was at stake. With the opening to foreign capital from 1956 on, and during the "Alliance for Progress" in the 1960s, the United States undertook numerous political and military interventions in the Caribbean (e.g., in Cuba in 1961 and in the Dominican Republic in 1964).

The Brazilian military coup of 1964 expelled President Goulart and cut ties with socialist countries, establishing a clear political and economic alliance with the United States. The final years of the Brazilian *Estado Novo*, Vargas's reelection in 1950, his suicide, and the years leading up to the military dictatorship were crucial for Brazilian politics and culture. For Freyre, whose political–ideological link with Getúlio Vargas's regime was always disguised as a personal friendship, these years were also transitional. His political influence as a delegate for Pernambuco and as a member of the parliament should not be ignored. For Freyre, to talk about culture, to define a Brazilian cultural subjectivity, was to discuss politics and, given the historical moment, Brazil's political intervention in the world.

In *New World at the Tropics*, Freyre inaugurates a discourse of cooperation with the United States and other countries based on pan-American values. His utopian tone is key to *tropicalismo*:

> With cultural compromise and a genius for combining civilized and indigenous values, (Brazilians) have been able, perhaps better than any other people of predominantly European origin, to adapt a European civilization to the tropics. (6)

> "Luso-tropical civilization" is an expression I have suggested to characterize what seems to me a particular form of behavior and a particular form of accomplishment of the Portuguese in the world: (the Portuguese man's) tendency to prefer the tropics for his extra-European expansion and his ability to successfully remain in the tropics—from both a cultural and an ecological point of view . . . (154)

In the context of a shifting global political map, Freyre was placing Brazil at the center of American and European cultures. Portugal was the creator of its values and the land of its past; Brazil was "the civilization of the future."

Though many of Freyre's conceptualizations of *tropicalismo* were published in the late 1950s, he began elaborating his definition of this term in 1937, as a Brazilian delegate for the *Congresso de Expansão do Mundo* (*Conference of Global Expansion*) in Lisbon. In six lectures later published as *Conferências na Europa* (1938), Freyre works with ideas of racial democracy and miscegenation that erase social and racial differences. In "Importância dos estudos da história social" (*The Importance of Social History Studies*) and "Açúcar: o Nordeste do Brasil" (*Sugar: The Northeast of Brazil*), Freyre calls for academic collaboration in comparative studies with areas similar to Brazil, such as Africa and the Caribbean: "Estudos sob critérios globais: americano, hispano-americano, ou hispano tropical" [*Studies according to global criteria; American, Hispano-American, or Hispano-Tropical* ("Importancia dos estudos transnacionais," 92)]. "Structures of feeling" and economic similarities between different tropical nations, deriving principally from colonization, are part of this earlier definition of *tropicalismo*. It is in the second and third moments, in the late 1950s and early 1960s, that *tropicalismo* becomes an ideological justification for the Portuguese dictatorship or, as some critics have argued, that Freyre lives his personal moment of "brilliance" in the eyes of Oliveira Salazar.

In "Em torno de um novo conceito de tropicalismo" (*On a New Concept of Tropicalism*), Freyre writes,

> Tropicalismo. Luso-tropicalismo. Velha antecipação portuguesa da idéia que hoje se aviva entre nórdicos, homens de estudo e homens de acção quer na Europa, quer nos Estados Unidos, de que o trópico é espaço fisicamente adequado para o desenvolvimento de civilizações aptas . . .

> (*Tropicalism. Luso-Tropicalism. The ancient Portuguese anticipation of the idea that is just now coming alive among the northerners, scholarly men and men of action, in Europe and the United States, that the tropics is the proper physical space for the development of apt civilizations . . . 21*)

On the one hand, it seems that Freyre is apologizing for the U.S. and European colonization of the tropics. On the other hand, this apology is problematized by his critique of U.S. imperialism in a lecture entitled "Uma política transnacional de cultura para o Brasil de hoje" (*A Transnational Cultural Policy for Today's Brazil*, 1960), in which he argues

> Somos dos que acreditam ser a política chamada anticolonialista, não diremos oficial, dos Estados Unidos, mas de alguns de seus políticos na Africa e no Oriente, uma preparação para seu domínio econômico e veladamente político em áreas tropicais . . .
>
> (*We are among those who believe that the so-called anticolonialist politics, not the official politics of the United States but that of certain of its politicians in Africa and the Orient, are a preparation for its veiled economic and political dominion in tropical regions*, 30).

Freyre seems to believe that a strong tropical culture could withstand postimperial displacements, particularly those initiated by the United States, and ultimately become an equal partner in global affairs. He employs Portugal's maritime, expansionist past as a cultural and political tool for overcoming the political forces of a bipolar world: "no futuro, o domínio do trópico augura o domínio global" (*in the future, the dominion of the tropics will predetermine global dominion*). Freyre uses terms such as *transplantação* (transplantation), *cordialidade* (cordiality), and *hibridação* (hybridization) to describe Portuguese colonization. In a lecture entitled "Aspectos da influência da mestiçagem" (*Aspects of the Influence of Miscegenation*), he writes,

> É uma zona sentimental e social—essa de relações de brancos com indígenas e com mestiços—para outros povos, cheia de atritos, de choques, de antagonismos os mais dramáticos, em que nos entendemos de maneira singular, os vários luso-descendentes hoje em grande maioria mestiços.
>
> (*It is a social and sentimental zone—this zone of the relations of whites with the indigenous and with mixed-race people—one that for other peoples would be full of misunderstandings, conflicts and antagonisms of the most dramatic sort, one in which we understand one another in a singular manner, the various luso-descendents who are today for the most part mixed-race*, 13).

Luso-tropical culture integrates instead of segregating, producing a transnational, democratic world through "structures of feeling." How did Gilberto Freyre see Africa and India and what were some of the reactions to his interpretations?

In *Aventura e Rotina* (*Adventure and Routine*, 1953) and *O Mundo Que o Português Criou* (*The World that the Portuguese Created*, 1952), Freyre articulates what Carlos Piñero Iñiguez has called a "parallel dream" for Brazilian and Portuguese politics (*Sueños Paralelos. Gilberto Freyre y el Lusotropicalismo*, 1999). If the intellectuals affiliated with the Portuguese regime looked to the past to emphasize Portugal's glorious sea expeditions to Asia, Africa, and America, Freyre focused on Brazil, situating Africa and Asia as "the Eastern frontier" for commercial and cultural exchange. As Piñero Iñiguez shows, Freyre's relationship to *salazarismo* before the 1960s was irregular and difficult to read, since many of the ideas he articulated during this time were paraphrased, discussed out of context, and combined in contradictory ways with the ideas espoused by the "intellectuals" affiliated with the *Estado Novo Português*.

As Portugal was already in economic ruin, a future commercial alliance with the ex-colonies was crucial for the regime's survival. For Freyre, it was Brazil rather than Portugal that was the land of the future, the site for an economic miracle. In the name of "o mundo que o português criou" (*the world that the Portuguese created*), Freyre stressed the Portuguese geographical discoveries. He celebrated Portugal's language, its Catholicism, its miscegenation. But he did so to stress values related to the Brazilian political present. Whereas in *Aventura e Rotina* Freyre addresses Indian and African "others," his emphasis is nonetheless upon Brazilian culture, and particularly its *mesticagem*. He *re-vê* (re-sees) African and Asian reality with "Brazilian eyes," filtering details subjectively. For instance, rather than cast language as a marker of difference, he identifies the Portuguese idiom as a homogeneous factor of integration which unites all *luso-descendentes* in spite of its "creolized versions." He also situates sexuality—and its effect, the "mixing of races and cultures"—as a great equalizer of Portuguese civilization.

In *Aventura e Rotina*, and particularly in the pages dedicated to Freyre's African tour, a tone of uncomfortable deception and sadness nonetheless emerges. Freyre's romantic expectations of *mestiço* societies are disappointed by the realities he witnesses in the African colonies. In Angola, Guiné Bissau, and Moçambique, he encounters rigid economic and social segregation between blacks and whites, tribal divisions, and colonial slavery. Still, in Freyre's unique sociological fashion, he displaces many of these realities with a "romantic" view of the ex-colonies that combines with an air of disillusionment.

Though Freyre was well received in Cape Verde, he remained there for only three days and dedicated only seventeen pages of his journal to this visit. Freyre had great expectations of the "lusotropical" character of Cape Verdian culture—particularly its cultural and literary proximity to the Brazilian northeast—that were disappointed upon arrival. For Freyre, Cape Verde's *mestiço* society had not functioned as it did in Brazil, since its *mulatos* were "darker than Brazilian ones" and many aspects of its African culture remained untouched by social whitening. Contradicting his affirmation of equality among "luso-descendentes," he displaces Cape Verdeans by emphasizing their "imitative" character. Freyre's remarks that "a cultura caboverdiana é imitativa da brasileira" (*Cape Verdean culture is imitative of Brazilian culture*), that *criolo* dialect "é excessivo e repugnante" (*is excessive and repugnant*) and that "não há futuro para Cabo Verde" (*there is no future for Cape Verde*) were received angrily by Cape Verdean intellectuals (Iñiguez, 293). The Cape Verdean writer Baltazar Lopes responded indignantly to Freyre's remarks in a Radio Barlavento program, later published as *Cabo Verde Visto por Gilberto Freyre* (1952): "Cabo Verde não é nem Africa, nem é Portugal, nem muito menos é afro-português. É mais que nada uma identidade própria, e original, socialmente específica" (*Cape Verde is neither Africa, nor Portugal, nor much less Afro-Portuguese. It is, more than anything, a distinct, original and socially specific identity*, Iñiguez, 299).[1]

During the late 1960s and 1970s, Freyre plays down the "tropicalist" character of *Luso* cultures to situate Brazil in relation to other "hispanotropical" Latin American countries. He organizes "lusotropicalist" conferences at the Federal University of Pernambuco dedicated entirely to the analysis of Brazilian society. Freyre insists that Brazil shares a particular historical tradition with the rest of Latin America: "a experiência do europeu com o saber e a experiência indígenas" (*the European's experience combined with indigenous knowledge and experience*, 35–36). Due to this shared tradition, Brazil should open itself culturally and politically to Latin America to find original solutions to its problems. It is thus that *tropicalismo* shifts from *luso-* to *hispano-tropical*:

> Nós, os povos hispano-tropicais que nos estendemos pela América, pela África e pelo Oriente, como nações uns, como quase nações outros, todos formando um complexo cultural que é um dos mais fortes e significativos do mundo de hoje, conservemo-nos alheios à nossa força e à base da nossa força, à nossa missão que é de oferecermos ou antes sermos, uma terceira solução para os problemas de relações entre europeus e não europeus, entre a Europa e os trópicos, entre as civilizações européias e as civilizacões não européias.

> ( *We, the hispano-tropical peoples who extend throughout America, Africa and the Orient, some as nations, others as semi-nations, all forming one of the strongest and most significant cultural complexes in today's world, will conserve ourselves beyond our might and grounded in our might, in our mission that is to offer or rather to make ourselves into a third solution for the problems between Europeans and non-Europeans, between Europe and the tropics, between European civilizations and non-European civilizations, 57*).

The so-called third world becomes the creator of a third space or solution for a bipolar world. In the name of culture, and of a Brazilian cultural subjectivity, a shared political knowledge for Latin America is born.

## *Tropicalismo* Now

Gilberto Freyre continued to theorize tropicalism in the fields of politics, art, science, and society until his death in 1987. The cultural basis of his thinking, consistently attacked by his critics, provides a new paradigm for understanding the economic and social inequalities of the globalized world. As Néstor García Canclini and Renato Ortiz have argued, *mundialização* and *globalización imaginada* are not for everyone. Transnational business and media corporations have the lead, displacing ethnic and cultural identities in such a manner that the representation of the personal histories and daily lives of these displaced peoples is of utmost urgency. Processes of displacement and the relationship of "otherness" to citizenship—vis-à-vis race, gender, sexuality, or class—are still on the table. Scholars in the humanities and social sciences have rescued terms such as "transculturation" and "tropicalism" as a means for understanding the presence of these "others" in the so-called multicultural United States. Employed in the distorted mirror of U.S. society, the theoretical use of these terms is necessarily altered.

Frances Aparicio and Susana Chávez—Silverman's *Tropicalizations: Transcultural Representations of Latinidad* (1997) inaugurates a form of "border thinking" that issues from the colonizer–colonized model while identifying forms of agency in the margins and questioning fixed dialectics. The term "tropicalization," coined not by Freyre but by U.S. Puerto Rican poet Víctor Hernández Cruz, allows us to "embrace not only the Caribbean but places such as México, Latin America and the United States" and to include "the dynamics of the colony from the space and the perspective of the colonized and use it as a tool that foregrounds the transformative cultural agency of the subaltern subject" (2). It thus becomes possible for tropicalized subjectivities to subvert racist, colonialist ideologies from within. Though we must take care in adapting social science terms such as *tropicalismo* and "tropicalization" to distinct critical contexts, we should continue to discuss these concepts, especially Freyre's perspective "from the tropics." In this New World order, we can look to the contradictions of national–transnational models of cultural identity such as Freyre's not only for a better understanding of the contexts in which they emerged but also for what they tell us about our contemporary "differential" modernities.

## NOTES

\* This essay is part of a chapter of my forthcoming book entitled *Travestismos culturales: literatura y etnografía en Cuba y Brasil* (Pittsburgh: Editorial Iberoamericana), in which I analyze the works of Gilberto Freyre and Fernando Ortiz, and trace their influences on several Brazilian and Cuban novels and ethnographies. Do not quote without the author's permission.

1. Intellectuals such as Amílcar Cabral and Mário Pinto de Andrade contested many such Freyrean "lusotropicalist" theories in the years before and after the wars of decolonization.

## WORKS CITED

Aparicio, Frances and Susana-Chávez Silverman, eds. *Tropicalizations: Transcultural Representations of Latinidad*. Hanover: University Press of New England, 1997.

Arroyo, Jossianna. *Travestismos culturales: literatura y etnografía en Cuba y Brasil*. Pittsburgh: Editorial Iberoamericana, 2003.

Freyre, Gilberto. *Aventura e rotina: sugestões de uma viagem à procura das constantes portuguesas de caráter e ação*. Rio de Janeiro: José Olympio, 1980.

———. "Em torno de um novo conceito de tropicalismo." Conferência pronunciada na sala dos Capelos da Universidade de Coimbra, 24 de Janeiro de 1952. Coimbra: Editora Limitada, 1952.

———. *O mundo que o português criou. Conferências na Europa*. Rio de Janeiro: Jose Olympio, 1940.

———. *New World in the Tropics: The Culture of Modern Brazil*. New York: Alfred A. Knopf, 1959.

———. *O Brasileiro entre os outros hispanos: afinidades, contrastes e possíveis futuros nas suas inter-relações*. Rio de Janeiro: José Olympio Ed, 1975.

———. "Introdução." *Um brasileiro em terras portuguesas. Introdução a uma possível luso-tropicologia, acompanhada de conferências e discursos proferidos em Portugal e em terras lusitanas e ex-lusitanas da Ásia, da África e do Atlântico*. Rio de Janeiro: Livraria José Olympio Ed., 1953.

Freyre, Gilberto. "Uma política transnacional para o Brasil de hoje." *Revista Brasileira de Estudos Políticos*. Faculdade de Direito de Minas Gerais, 1960.

García Canclini, Néstor. *La globalización imaginada*. Buenos Aires: Paidós, 1999.

Levi-Strauss, Claude. *Tristes trópiques*. Trans. John and Doreen Weightman. London: Jonathan Cape, 1973.

Magalhães, Agamenon. *O Nordeste Brasileiro*. Recife: Editora ASA, 1985.

Mignolo, Walter D. *Local Histories/Global Designs, Coloniality, Subaltern Knowledges, and Border Thinking*. New Jersey: Princeton University Press, 2000.

Ortiz, Fernando. *Contrapunteo cubano del tabaco y el azúcar*. La Habana: Jesús Montero, 1940.

Piñero Iñiguez, Carlos. *Sueños paralelos. Gilberto Freyre y el lusotropicalismo. Identidad, cultura y política en Brasil y Portugal*. Argentina: Centro de Política Exterior, 1999.

Stepan, Nancy L. *Picturing Tropical Nature*. New York: Cornell University Press, 2001.

# CHAPTER 8

# Hybridity and *Mestizaje*: Sincretism or Subversive Complicity? Subalternity from the Perspective of the Coloniality of Power[*]

*Ramón Grosfoguel*

Any intercultural or north/south dialogue must begin by identifying the coordinates of global power. One cannot hope for transparent communication, or aspire to an ideal communication community a la Habermas, without identifying the relations of global power and the silenced, excluded "others," ignored or exterminated by global coloniality of power (Quijano, 2000). Any intercultural dialogue must take as its premise that we do not live in a horizontal world of cultural relations. Horizontality implies a false equality that does not contribute in any way to a productive dialogue between north and south. We should begin by recognizing that we live in a world in which relations between cultures are vertical, between dominated and dominators, colonized and colonizers. This verticality institutes important problems. One of them is how northern privileges—won through the exploitation and domination of global coloniality—impact communication, intercultural exchange and dialogue with the south. Before any such dialogue can occur, one must begin by recognizing the inequalities of power and the complicity of the north in the south's exploitation.

The geopolitics of knowledge is central to this discussion. No one is thinking from an ethereal space or from the perspective of God. We are all thinking from a specific place in the relations of world global power. The question of "from where" one is speaking conditions that which is visible and invisible; this absent trace constitutes us in our incessant invisibility. I refer to the matrix of power that, following the Peruvian sociologist Aníbal Quijano, I will call "global coloniality." It becomes anachronistic to speak of colonial relations in a world that is apparently decolonized. But as we witness the continuation of the coloniality of power, those relations remain key to any discussion of an intercultural north/south dialogue. For example, global power coloniality changes how we understand intercultural, north/south processes as much with respect to the south as in relation to the north. I refer to that which recently has been called *mestizaje*, hybridity or cultural mixing in the encounter between Europeans and non-Europeans inside and outside of metropolitan centers. Seen from a Eurocentric perspective—from the hegemonic side of colonial difference—these syncretic processes appear to reflect horizontal cultural relations. But seen from the subaltern side of colonial difference, they constitute the political, cultural, and social strategies of subaltern subjects who, from subordinated positions of power—that is, from within a system of vertical intercultural relations—interject epistemologies, cosmologies, and political strategies that are alternatives to Eurocentrism and pose ways of resisting power relations. To call this "syncretism" is an act of symbolic violence that reduces these processes to the myth of horizontal, egalitarian cultural integration. If we don't wish to commit the ridiculous error of the Spanish colonizers who, in the seventeenth, eighteenth, and nineteenth centuries believed they had colonized the African slaves when they witnessed them adoring Catholic saints, it will be necessary to look at hybridization and *mestizaje* as political–cultural strategies understood from the subaltern side of colonial difference. But first it is necessary to clarify what is meant by global coloniality.

## GLOBAL COLONIALITY

The geoculture or global ideologies of the capitalist modern/colonial world system that are still current to this day originated during European colonial expansion in the sixteenth century. Contrary to the way it has been traditionally conceptualized by bourgeois economics and orthodox Marxism, historical capitalism has been a global system since its commencement in the sixteenth century.[1] It is reductive to think of historical capitalism as a purely economic system circumscribed by a nation-state. Historical capitalism has consisted in a network of global oppression and colonial power since its beginning in the sixteenth century. European colonial expansion constructed various global hierarchies at once. The temporal simultaneity of the emergence of these global hierarchies eliminates the conceptions of infrastructure and superstructure that inform many Marxist theories. It invalidates Western conceptualizations that deny the contemporaneity of the various regions' incorporation, using the rhetoric of advanced versus primitive, developed versus undeveloped countries.

European colonial expansion simultaneously institutionalized and normalized on a global level the supremacy of a class, an ethnic-racial group, a gender, a sexuality, a particular type of state organization, a spirituality, a type of institutionalization of knowledge, a language, and an economy oriented toward the accumulation of capital on a global scale. One cannot separate these processes. The word "capitalism" is in fact deceptive because it calls to mind an economic system, when in reality it transcends economic relations, instituting racial, sexual, gender, spiritual, linguistic, and epistemological relations, articulated through a matrix of colonial power that establishes the biological and/or cultural superiority of populations of European origin over non-European populations. Historical capitalism operates according to the following hierarchies: first, an international division of work composed of metropolitan centers, peripheries subordinated to those centers and semi-peripheries that have a central relation to peripheral regions and a peripheral relation to certain centers; second, an interstate system of dominant and subordinated, metropolitan and peripheral states, corresponding in most cases to the hierarchy of the international division of labor and organized around the fiction of the nation-state; third, a class hierarchy divided by capital and the different forms of exploited labor; fourth, an ethnic-racial hierarchy in which white Europeans dominate non-European ethno-racial groups constructed as culturally and/or biologically "inferior others;" fifth, a gender hierarchy in which men have more power and infiltrate social relations with a virile, patriarchal *machista* construction of national, political, and/or cultural discursivity;[2] sixth, a sexual hierarchy in which heterosexuality is privileged over homosexuality; seventh, a spiritual hierarchy in which Christianity is privileged over other religions; eighth, an epistemic hierarchy in which European knowledge is privileged over non-European knowledge through a global network of universities.

These eight hierarchies are historically interlaced. I have separated them for purely analytical reasons. They constitute historical capitalism rather than the ideal capitalisms of orthodox Marxist textbooks or developmentalist ideologies. White, capitalist, heterosexual, military,

Christian, European man expanded his domain across the globe, taking with him and imposing the privileges of his racial, military, class, sexual, epistemic, spiritual, and gender positionality. These diverse, interlaced colonialities are central to the hierarchies and global ideologies that still persist on a planetary scale in the twenty-first century. Homophobia, racism, sexism, classism, militarism, Christian-centrism, and Eurocentrism are all born of capitalist, masculinized, whitened, heterosexualized colonial power. For instance, the racialization of the American Indians cannot be comprehended without understanding homophobia. For most of the American indigenous, homosexual relationships were a part of their quotidian sexual practices. European colonization pathologized such relations as part of a strategy of racialization to demonstrate the inferiority of the indigenous and the need to convert them to Christianity.[3] Neither can one understand militarism and political repression as the means to resolving social conflict without understanding white, masculinist, heterosexist supremacy.

Globalization—understood as the mobility of people, capital, merchandise, ideology, culture, and ideas across national frontiers—has a history of five hundred and ten years. The new element in the last thirty years of the colonial/capitalist world-system is the autonomy won by multinational and nation-state corporations.[4] The multinationals mobilized their investments across national frontiers without even the central states being able to regulate the flow of capital. Given this context, it would be a nineteenth-century fantasy to conceive of economic development in small pockets of national capitalism, or of socialism in peripheral countries whose historical legacy has been of subordination to center-capitalist countries. This phenomenon places in question "developmentalist" ideologies and the liberal bourgeois myth of the "sovereignty of the nation-states," among the pillars of modernity.

Nation-states lose more control of the socioeconomic processes within their frontiers with every passing day.[5] The global capitalism of the borderless economy *inverts* inside/outside, interior/exterior and national/foreign, undoing the dualisms of "anti-imperialist" thought and the "bourgeois" notion of sovereignty as a step toward self-sustained, auto-sufficient development. As a result, the notion of a radical rupture that permits us to locate ourselves outside of the capitalist world-system to create a new society ("socialism") is in crisis; even more importantly, so is the metaphysical image of a moderate rupture with the United States and Europe that would permit us to locate ourselves in a "free, sovereign" space outside of its structures of political and global economic power, inserting the periphery in a new way into the international division of labor. There is no outside— or rather, on the level of political economy, all of us are inside the system. Even worse, any attempt to locate oneself outside is immediately suffocated by commercial blockades, military aggressions, World Bank freezes on credit and loans, and the imposition of onerous conditions for the payment of foreign debt. This takes us to the question of what has been mis-termed Latin American and Caribbean "independence," and of what we understand by decolonization.

## DECOLONIZATION OR RECOLONIZATION?

The so-called independence of the peripheral countries of Latin America and especially the Caribbean, from the nineteenth century on, has been one of the most effective myths in the reproduction of "developmentalist" and "national sovereignty" ideologies. The region's problems are constructed as internal nation-state problems without any connection to the exploitation and domination of the capitalist/colonial world-system. Nationalist "rights" and "lefts" reduce colonial relations to a juridical–political relationship, which they conceive as terminated as soon as the territories are legally constituted as independent states. But colonial relations are not merely juridical. If we conceive of colonial relations as a political, economic, sexual, spiritual, and epistemological relationship of ethno-racial domination, then the mis-termed "independent" republics of Latin America and the Caribbean are still territories that need to be decolonized.[6] It would be better to characterize them, following Aníbal Quijano (2000), as "independent colonies."

In the first place, the peripheral nation-states of Latin America and especially the Caribbean are neocolonies. The third world independence movements of the last hundred years never inverted the global hierarchies created by four hundred years of European world colonization. The peripheral nations continue to be subordinated through the international division of labor, and the metropolitan states' and corporations' interstate system of economic, political, and military dominion.[7] The illusion that these states are "sovereign" because they decided their destiny freely and independently of the political and economic relations of force of the capitalist world-system is one of the most important myths of world capitalism.[8] It is not enough to say that "sovereignty" was always limited and that it always operated on behalf of the economically and militarily more powerful states of the capitalist world-system. The peripheries never counted with the sovereignty of the centers, having always been submitted and subordinated to the metropolises through diverse mechanisms of colonial and neocolonial coercion that include everything from direct military invasions to commercial embargoes.

In the case of the Caribbean nation-states, sovereignty was never real. The United States' and transnational corporations' geopolitical military and economic control of the region make this notion a joke in poor taste. The coup d'état implemented by the CIA to the Arbenz governement of Guatemala in 1954, the invasion of French troops in Martinique in 1959, the invasion financed by the CIA in Cuba in Bahia de Cochinos in 1961, the destabilization of the Chedhdi Jagan governement of Guyana in 1963, the U.S. invasion of the Dominican Republic to topple the constitutional government in 1965, the invasion of Dutch troops in Curação in 1969, the destabilization of the Manley government in the 1970s, the war on the Nicaraguan Sandinistas in the 1980s, the U.S. invasion of Grenada in 1984, of Panamá in 1990 and of Haiti in 1995 are recent examples that speak for the false sovereignty of the (autonomous or independent) neo-colonies of our region. At the beginning of the twenty-first century, the illusion of sovereignty—that is, the myth of the independence of the peripheral states—is substantially debilitated not only by imperialist military hegemony in the Caribbean region that impedes real political independence but also by the absence of control over the mobility of capital that crosses limitlessly across national borders.

I thus sustain that we have moved from global colonialism to global coloniality. Global colonialism describes the period of European colonial expansion between 1492 and 1945. Since 1945, we have seen the fall of the colonial administrations with the third world anticolonial wars. I describe this as a period of global coloniality, since the global colonial hierarchies between Europeans and non-Europeans, constructed through four hundred and fifty years of colonialism throughout the world, have remained intact in spite of the fact that the colonial administrations have been eradicated almost all across the planet. Global colonialism is a period of colonial relations with colonial administrations while global coloniality is a period of colonial relations without colonial administrations. The historical–social conditions of the last sixty years (1945–2004) of global coloniality were made possible by four hundred and fifty years of global colonialism (1492–1945). Without global colonialism there would not today be global coloniality.

Second, the mis-termed "independent countries" of the Americas (and I now include North America) are territories yet to be decolonized for they are experiencing what Aníbal Quijano calls the "coloniality of power."[9] Juridically, Latin America, the Caribbean and North America are separated from France, Great Britain, and Spain, but the ethno-racial hierarchies constructed through years of colonial subordination remain intact. Creole whites, in the case of Latin America, and "elite browns," in the case of the Caribbean, continue to wield social, political, and economic power over blacks, indigenous, *mestizos*, *mulattos*, Asians, and other racialized groups in the new neocolonial states. The ideology of the nation-state is constructed on top of the ideology of the nation, a fictional unity of sovereign individuals brought together as an "imaginary community" on the basis of a common culture and/ or blood ties.[10] In general, the elites that control state power belong to the dominant race or ethnicity. It is they who define which culture or "blood tie" will be invented as the criteria for belonging to the nation, criteria thereupon applied to the individuals submitted to the power of the state. Those ethnic or racial groups who do not enter into this definition of nation are excluded, subjugated, assimilated, or exterminated depending on the particular history of each nation-state. The national projects as they have been historically conceived are at heart a racist, ethnocentrist, sexist, and homophobic exclusion of subordinated others. It is not the case that the nation is "en la orilla"[11] but rather that the nation is always an *orilla*,[12] a border that defines who are included in or excluded from it.

In the colonial world, the nation has an ambiguous character. On the one hand, it constructs a fiction of homogeneous identity through anticolonial struggle while on the other, it installs the modern, Eurocentric ideology of the nation-state. In order to constitute a space of homogeneous, common identity, the foundational discourses of the "nation" invent *orillas*, borders that define who belongs and who does not belong to the "nation." The national project is a perennial effort to constantly erase its *orilla*, reifying the homogeneous space that is constructed by excluding others. Those others are racial and sexual groups who are pathologized in opposition to the national project, a discourse constituted by patriarchal, *machista* images of the heterosexual man. The nation is an effort to border-ize other groups so that the myth of homogeneity may be reproduced. Since at this point in history the nation's *orillas* cannot be hidden, the pretense of national homogeneity is in crisis. The argument that "the nation is in an *orilla*" is the rhetoric of those who wish to reestablish the exclusionary homogeneity of the nation. At root, this is an authoritarian, colonialist discourse that sustains or reinstates racial hierarchies. This is made clear by its privileging of the Hispanic character of the nation; defining a country of blacks and mulattos like Puerto Rico as "Hispanic" reproduces ethno-racial hierarchies installed by colonialism.[13] This is a foreboding preview of colonial power in the future neocolonial republic.

In this sense, the United States as much as the Latin American and Caribbean republics requires economic–political as well as social and cultural decolonization. "Decolonize" acquires new meaning that transcends the mere jurido-political problem. It strives to overcome coloniality not only juridically but also socially so as to decolonize epistemologies, sexuality, gender relations, politics, economy, and ethno-racial hierarchies. All of these problems are articulated in an interrelated way in the world matrix of colonial power that privileges Europeans and Euro-Americans over non-Europeans. In summary, the false peripheral republics of the Americas suffer from a double coloniality: (1) the dominion of ethno-racial elites and (2) the location of political, economic, and military control in the metropolitan centers.

Is Europe exempted from the need for decolonization? One of the great Eurocentric myths is that decolonization is a third world process in which the first world does not need to participate. Europe and the United States, world colonial powers for various centuries, and metropolitan centers that today benefit from the exploitation and domination of the peripheral countries, produce global coloniality through the international division of labor, and retain racist colonial ideologies that inform their relations to the third world both inside and outside their borders. The third world within European and U.S. frontiers are the migrant Africans, Arabs, Caribbeans, Latin Americans, and Asians of their ex-colonies. These populations are the periphery in the interior of the centers: the exploited, dominated colonial workforce Europe needs in order to support a privileged lifestyle in relation to the rest of the world. Part of the European colonial inheritance is reflected in the racism and neo-fascism that characterize political debate. On the other hand, the third world outside the national frontiers of the North are the peripheral nations who provide *materia prima*, merchandise, and cheap labor for the metropolitan investors.

Decolonization implies an intervention, within and without Europe, of the racial, political, gender, and economic hierarchies constructed by European colonialism of the world. In the Caribbean, we have Aimé Cesaire's legacy; Cesaire, who understood that the false independence of the Caribbean islands is a form of neocolonial colonization, impelled the annexation of the French Antilles in an effort to extend the borders of citizenship rights and state welfare resources enjoyed by metropolitan citizens. His decolonizing project did not stop there. On the cultural level, Cesaire developed a struggle to recognize both the African roots of the Martinican nation and the equal citizenship of black Caribbeans within the French state. Instead of allowing the neocolonial subordination of a false republic in which Europeans and Euro-Americans continue to control and exploit local economies—without the expense of the colonial administrations—Cesaire fought for decolonization via the transference of those same civil, social, and democratic rights recognized for the metropolitan French to racialized colonial populations.[14]

The paradox is that, today, those Caribbean countries that did not attain independence have a better quality of life than those that through great blood and sweat became independent. Cesaire's framework is nonetheless not reproducible in the rest of the third world. No European country would at this point accept incorporating any of its ex-colonies, extending to them equal citizenship with the metropolitan populations, and I doubt that the populations of the third world have any desire to be reintegrated by the metropolitan countries even with the offer of equal citizenship. Still, Cesaire's model for Martinique dramatizes a great difference between the nonindependent Caribbean and the independent Caribbean that is crucial for any discussion about decolonizing global coloniality.

If it is true that in both Caribbeans there is exploitation and the extraction of wealth from the South to the North, in the nonindependent Caribbean there is also a distribution of wealth from the North to the South, via transferences through access to metropolitan citizenship. The French, Dutch, United States and some of the British islands, all nonindependent territories, receive great sums of metropolitan transfers. These are the modern colonies of the new type wherein there is a mechanism of distribution of wealth from North to South that does not exist in the independent Caribbean. The conclusion is not that we need to convert ourselves back into metropolitan colonies, but that any process of global decolonization must create mechanisms for the distribution of wealth that halts once and for all the ceaseless transference of wealth from South to North. This is the only way to confront the problem of global wealth inequality and the polarization of exploited third world countries and metropolitan countries that enjoy a high quality of life by commercially and militarily appropriating and expropriating the periphery's wealth.

## NEITHER WESTERN NOR THIRD WORLD FUNDAMENTALISMS

With the arguments maintained thus far I do not wish to establish an anti-Western essentialism that sustains binary oppositions according to Eurocentrist logic and reproduces a variant of (nationalist) "third world fundamentalism." Given the history of European colonial expansion and its permeation across the globe since the end of the nineteenth century, there is no absolute outside of the West. But this does not mean that there are no alternatives to Eurocentrism and Westernism. There are border cosmologies and strategies for displacement that provide alternatives to Eurocentrist fundamentalism (Christian, Zionist, etc.) and Third World fundamentalism (whether Islamic or another type). This is what Walter Mignolo, following the theoretical production of chicanos in the United States (Alarcón, 1983; Anzaldua, 1987; Saldívar, 1997), has called "border epistemologies," or what Enrique Dussel (2002) has called "transmodernity" (2000).

Recognizing that there is no absolute outside of the West does not mean that we must legitimate Westernism and Eurocentric fundamentalism, concluding that there are no alternatives to the capitalist world-system. This logic ends up romanticizing the West and Europe as it honors third worldism. In other words, trying not to succumb to a binary inversion of terms, the postmodernists end up reproducing the dominant European logic, privileging the hegemonic pole of the binary opposition (in this case Europe and the United States) rather than effectively displacing both poles of the binary opposition. The postmodernists reproduce what Walter Mignolo, following Enrique Dussel, calls "a Eurocentric critique of eurocentrism" (2000). Neither imperial Eurocentrism nor third world nationalism is an adequate alternative. Neither represents a democratic strategy, or a strategy of alterity, for displacing binary oppositions. One must look to "border thinking" (Mignolo, 2000), to "transmodernity" (Dussel, 2000), to "subversive complicity" (Grosfoguel, 1996, 2002), to the "miraculous weapons" (Cesaire, 1983), and to "transculturation" (Ortiz, 1995) for strategies for displacing Western power relations.

These non-Western political strategies have been practiced by social movements and subaltern subjects throughout the world—by Puerto Ricans, Martinicans, indigenous peoples, Afro-North Americans, Afro-Caribbeans, Islamic Feminists, Zapatistas, the "madres de mayo" (Argentina), and other subjects located on the subaltern side of colonial difference. These means of resistance and subsistence within a hierarchical and unequal relation of power have existed since colonial times. Slaves' prayers to Catholic saints are strategies of hibridization and *mestizaje* that have nothing to do with "syncretism." The hybridization practiced on the subaltern side of colonial difference represents "subversive complicity," "border thinking," and "transculturation;" subsistence and resistance in the face of colonial power. The Catholic saints were "transculturated" and "transmodernized" so as to subvert and redefine them within a global, non-European cosmology. Each saint was converted into an African God.

Alternatives to Eurocentric (imperialist) and third world (nationalist) fundamentalisms exist. Because we do not see them—due to limited, distorted mass media coverage or because they are hidden behind the dark glasses of Eurocentrism—does not mean they do not exist. The postmodernist reduction of *mestizaje* and hybridity to syncretism reproduces the absurdity and naivite of the Spanish colonizers who equated slaves' prayers to images of Catholic saints with "assimilation" and "Christianization." What was occurring behind slaves' hybrid appropriation of the images of the Catholic Church escaped Eurocentric lenses. The "inexistence of alternatives to the west" is another index of Western epistemological limitation, of the incapacity to break with Eurocentrism. Slaves "transculturated," "borderized," and "transmodernized" the images of the Catholic saints within an African cosmology. Santa Bárbara was converted into Changó and the Virgen de la Caridad into the Cobre de Yemayá.

These processes do not belong to the past. They are vigorously and powerfully manifest in the strategies of colonial subjects within and without the metropolis. Music, for instance, provides one of the most powerful metaphors for border thinking. One can appreciate this by looking at African rhythm's subversion of hegemonic music from within. The synchopated rhythm of African origin, known in the Caribbean as the "clave," has a restructuring effect, Africanizing instruments and musical melodies of European origin. The "clave" is the silence that constitutes the sound from an absence that is never present. The clave is silent because no one necessarily marks it though all musicians follow it. Yuri Buenaventura, the Columbian *sonero* radicated in Paris, has a song entitled "Ne me Quitte Pas," originally by Jacques Brel, just as La India, the Puerto Rican *salsera* in New York, has a song entitled "Ese Hombre," originally by Rocío Jurado. These artists Africanize and transculturate the songs with the synchopated rhythm of the "clave." This is comparable to slaves' prayers to the Catholic saints; no one necessarily says they are practicing African religion/cosmology though they are all doing so. It is the difference between "hacer diciendo" (doing by saying) and "decir haciendo" (saying by doing). The first acts by emitting an enunciation, while the second acts in silence.

In summary, I agree with critiques of the essentializing effects of monolithic divisions between "West" and "East." "Border thinking" constitutes an alternative to this problem. In a world where there is no outside of the West, how do we displace, rather than invert, Eurocentrism? What forms of thought, of subaltern cosmology and sociability, offer alternatives to hegemonic thinking and Western sociability without falling into third world nationalistic fundamentalism? This is the challenge we have before us. If third world essentialism is not the answer, resigning ourselves to the deterministic idea that "there is no alternative to Eurocentrism and Westernism" is not a solution either. These are both absolutist responses that leave intact the binary oppositions and hierarchies of power produced by global coloniality. I take the fact that there is no absolute outside of the West as a point of departure for searching for a way out, through "border thinking" that resignifies Western hegemonic discourses from subaltern, non-Western epistemic locations. This is the thinking of subaltern subjects who strategize from the subordinated side of colonial difference without establishing a pure outside of the West, as do Islamic, indigenist, and other third-world fundamentalists. Martin Luther King is an example of border thinking. He took the hegemonic discourse of "equality" and resignified it, extending it to blacks and native Americans. The Zapatistas are another example of border thinking; from traditional indigenous locales, they resignify "democracy" with the concepts of "mandar obediciendo" (ruling by obeying) and "somos iguales porque somos diferentes" (we are equal because we are different).

It is not about leaving the definition of modernity in the hands of Eurocentrists but, rather, resignifying it beyond the limits that the West has imposed upon the world. I have called this strategy "subversive complicity" (Grosfoguel, 1996, 2002). It is important to point out that "border thinking," "subversive complicity," and "transmodernity" are not equivalent to syncretism or *mestizaje*. They are about something very different, something not reducible to the colonial language of anthropologists. In border thinking, there is no assumption of horizontalness between cultures but, instead, a vertical relation wherein the West is dominant. Border thinking is an internal subversion of colonial difference. The notion of the "border" is not accidental. It describes rupture with third world and Eurocentric fundamentalisms with the goal of decolonizing the imaginary and conceiving of more just possible alternatives to the modern/colonial world-system.

NOTES

*   This essay was translated from Spanish by Alexandra Isfahani-Hammond.

1.  See Immanuel Wallerstein, *The Modern World-System I* (1974); *The Modern World-System II* (1979); *The Modern World-System III* (1989).
2.  See Wallerstein, *The Capitalist World Economy* (1979); Edward Said, *Orientalism* (1979); Cynthia Enloe, *Bananas, Beaches and Bases* (1989).
3.  It's not that patriarchy was born in Europe but, rather, that in many colonized parts of the world patriarchy did not exist prior to European expansion—in other words, gender relationships were matriarchal or egalitarian. Where patriarchy existed, it was a system that operated according to a social logic that was very different from European patriarchy. One would thus have to look carefully at the specific manner in which European patriarchy was articulated in relation to the organization of gender relationships in each region colonized by Europe.
4.  Giovanni Arrighi, *The Long Twentieth Century* (1994); Octavio Ianni, *Teorias de Globalización* (1996).
5.  Ramón Gsorfoguel, "Suicidio o Redifinición," *El Nuevo Dia*, June 25, 1990: 55.
6.  Miguel Rojas Mix, *Los cien Nombres de America* (1991); Aníbal Quintano, "Colonialidad y Modernidad/ Racionalidad," *Perú Indígena* (1991) 29: 11–21; Aníbal Quintano, " 'Raza,' 'Etnia' y 'Nación' en Mariátegui: Cuestiones Abiertas" in *José Carlos Mariátegui y Europa: El Otro Aspecto del Descubrimiento*, ed. Roland Forgues (1993); Frantz Fanon, *Black Skin, White Masks* (1967).
7.  See the dependency literature of the following authors: André Gunder Frank, *Capitalismo y subdesarrollo en América Latina* (1970); Fernando H. Cardoso y Enzo Faletto, *Dependencia y Desarrollo en América Latina* (1969); Vania Bambirra, *El Capitalismo Dependiente Latinoamericano* (1974); Anne Macklintock, *Imperial Leather: Race, Gender and Sexuality in the Colonial Context* (1995); *Unthinking Eurocentrism: Multiculturalism and the Media* (1994).
8.  Immanuel Wallerstein, *After Liberalism* (1995, 93–107).
9.  For Quijano, coloniality is constructed through European expansion and implies a hierarchical doubling between (1) work and capital; and (2) Europeans and non-Europeans. See Aníbal Quijano, "Colonialidad y Modernidad/Racionalidad," 29(1991): 11–21;

Aníbal Quijano, " 'Raza', 'Etnia' y 'Nación' en Mariátegui: Cuestiones Abiertas."

10. Bennedict Anderson, *Imagined Communities* (1983); Immanuel Wallerstein, *After Liberalism* (1995), 72–92, 232–251.

11. Luis Fernando Coss, *La Nación "en la orilla"* (1996).

12. I owe this deconstructionist observation that the nation is always an "orilla" to Chloe S. Georas.

13. Recently published nationalist texts that represent this way of thinking include Luis Fernando Coss, *La Nación en la Orilla* (1996) and Juan Manuel Carrión, *La Voluntad de Nación* (1996).

14. Ernest Moutoussany, *Aimé Césaire: Député 'a l'Assemblée Nationale 1945–1993* (1994).

## Works Cited

Alarcón, Norma. "Chicana Feminist Literature: A Re-Vision through Malintzín/or Malintzín: Putting Flesh Back on the Object." In *This Bridge Called My Back: Writing by Radical Women of Color* ed. Cherríe Moraga and Gloria Anzaldúa. New York: Kitchen Table/Women of Color, 1983, 182–190.

Anderson, Benedict. *Imagined Communities*. London: Verso, 1983.

Anzaldúa, Gloria. *Borderlands/La Frontera: The New Mestiza*. San Francisco: Spinsters/Aunt Lute, 1987.

Arrighi, Giovanni. *The Long Twentieth Century*. New York: Verso, 1994.

Cesaire, Aimé. *The Collected Poetry*. Berkeley: University of California Press, 1983.

Coss, Luis Fernando. "La Nación en la Orilla (Respuesta a los Post-modernistas Pesimistas)." San Juan: Editorial Punto de Encuentro, 1996.

Dussel, Enrique. *Hacia una filosofía política crítica*. Bilbao, España: Editorial Desclé de Brouwer, 2002.

Enloe, Cynthia. *Bananas, Beaches and Bases*. Berkeley: University of California Press, 1989.

Grosfoguel, Ramón. "From Cepalismo to Neoliberalism: A World-System Approach to Conceptual Shifts in Latin America." *Review*, 19 (2) (1996): 131–154.

——— . *Colonial subjects. Puerto Ricans in a Global Perspective*. Berkeley: The University of California Press, 2002.

Gunder Frank, Andre. "Desenvolvimento do Subdesenvolvimento Latinoamericano." In *Monthly Review*, 18 (5), Sept. 1966.

Ianni, Octavio. *Teorias de la Globalización*. Mexico City: Veintiuno editores, 1996.

Mignolo, Walter. *The Darker Side of the Renaissance: Literacy, Territoriality and Colonization*. Ann Arbor: The University of Michigan Press, 1995.

——— . *Local Histories/Global Designs: Essays on the Coloniality of Power, Subaltern Knowledges and Border Thinking*. Princeton: Princeton University Press, 2000.

Ortiz, Fernando. *Cuban Counterpoint: Tobacco and Sugar.* Durham: Duke University Press, 1995.

Quijano, Aníbal. " 'Raza', 'Etnia' y 'Nación' en Mariátegui: Cuestiones Abiertas." In *José Carlos Mariátgui y Europa: El Otro Aspecto del Descubrimiento* ed. Roland Forgues. Lima, Perú: Empresa Editora Amauta S.A., 1993. 167–187.

Said, Edward. *Orientalism.* New York: Vintage Books, 1979.

Saldívar, José David. *Border Matters.* Berkeley: University of California Press, 1997.

Wallerstein, Immanuel. *After Liberalism.* New York: The New Press, 1995.

——— . *The Capitalist World-Economy.* Cambridge and Paris: Cambridge University Press and Editions de la Maison des Sciences de l'Homme, 1979.

——— . *The Modern World-System I.* New York: Academic Press, 1974.

——— *The Modern World-System II.* New York: Academic Press, 1990.

——— .*The Modern World-System III.* San Diego: Academic Press, 1989.

CHAPTER 9

# The Rhythm of Macumba: Lívio Abramo's Engagement with Afro-Brazilian Culture*

*Luiza Franco Moreira*

William Hayter's *About Prints* includes a woodcut by Brazilian artist Lívio Abramo (1903–1992) and assigns it a prominent place: Abramo's "Macumba" (1957) is the second illustration in a book that reproduces works by artists whose names we are quick to recognize—Picasso, Chagall, Henry Moore, and Max Ernst. Hayter, of course himself a key figure in the history of modern printmaking, explains that his book aims to present "a sampling of contemporary prints including some extreme experiments" in order to indicate "the enormous variety" of the field. He specifies that the prints chosen were often "provocative and little known" (v).

Abramo's prints were certainly little known to Hayter's international audience. Abramo studied printing with Hayter in his Atelier 17 in the early fifties, after winning a prize at the prestigious Salão Nacional de Belas Artes in Rio de Janeiro that funded his trip to Europe in 1950; according to Lélia Abramo, the award recognized both his illustrations for Afonso Arinos' *Pelo Sertão* and one of the prints in the series, *Macumba* (133). Though Abramo had been active both as a graphic artist and illustrator since the 1930s, around 1950 his career took a turn for the better, when he won this and other prestigious prizes. He is best known for the prints he made from the 1950s on, black-and-white woodcuts like the one reproduced by Hayter, which seem to balance abstraction and figuration, combining a wealth of graphic effects with a sure handling of rhythm and composition.

This chapter takes the woodcut reproduced by Hayter as a starting point for examining Abramo's achievement as a graphic artist and illustrator. As is often the case with Brazilian artists, Abramo's work takes shape in the twofold context of Modern Art, both internationally and within Brazil. (Brazilian Modernism, usually said to begin in the early 1920s, led to the renewal of most forms of artistic expression in the country.) The artwork for which Abramo is best known articulates a complex response to formal and cultural problems that were being explored at the time, both in Brazil and internationally. His early work as an illustrator helps us appreciate the complexity and balance that distinguish his art from the 1950s on. Since his illustrations call attention to questions that remain implicit rather than explicit in his art, they reveal unexpected dimensions not only of Abramo's talent but of his career itself.

The first part of this chapter looks at the woodcut reproduced in Hayter's *About Prints*, taking it as the focal point for a discussion of Abramo's graphic art. This print proposes new solutions to an enduring problem for Modernist art in Brazil, that of representing Afro-Brazilian culture. Exploring the boundaries of abstract and figurative art, Abramo finds an original approach to this old problem. We know well that the tension between abstraction and figuration lies at the center of postwar art in general. In Brazil, as Tadeu Chiarelli points out, this conflict often appears as the alternative between an abstract art characterized by its openness to international currents and a figurative art that develops from the work of an earlier generation of Brazilian Modernists. Lívio Abramo, Chiarelli emphasizes, is one of the Brazilian artists who fashioned an original "third" path that led to works of "strong artistic and aesthetic interest." In effect, Abramo's nearly abstract "Macumba" can be enjoyed as an exploration of composition, rhythm, light, and the craft of woodcutting, but it also calls attention to the issue of how to represent the Afro-Brazilian woman, a problem that had already been explored in the 1920s by Tarsila do Amaral in a well-known Modernist figurative painting.

The second part of this chapter focuses on Abramo's earlier work as an illustrator, and specifically on his illustrations for Cassiano Ricardo's *Marcha para Oeste* (1940). It devotes special attention to a picture that has a clear thematic affinity with the artwork reproduced by Hayter, because it includes the image of an Afro-Brazilian woman in the foreground. Unlike "Macumba" and, indeed, unlike most of Abramo's artistic prints, his illustrations for this text are unambiguously figurative. His talent as a storyteller and his sense of humor come to the fore in images that tell a complex story clearly and quickly. One of the most interesting revelations of Abramo's illustrations for *Marcha para Oeste* is the artist's commitment to socialism. These prints bear witness to his inventiveness and courage in not only producing but also publishing works that reflect a socialist perspective in the repressive political context of 1940s Brazil.

My conclusion to this chapter addresses the problem of how to best comprehend Abramo's overall achievement. The question is not so much that of describing a trajectory the artist might have followed from his earlier work as an illustrator—committed to Left revolutionary projects—to the sophisticated graphic art of his maturity. Though he is most often remembered for his production from the 1950s on, Abramo had worked consistently and well as a graphic artist since the 1930s. On the other hand, he never abandoned his interest in "committed art." In 1988, a few years before his death, Abramo produced a series of drawings entitled "Os Frisos do Parternon" (*Brasil-Paraguai*) that returned to the theme of São Paulo poverty, which had been central to his work in the 1930s. Rather than construct a chronological narrative of Abramo's development, this chapter relies on a discussion of two works, each of a different nature and created at distinct moments in the artist's career, to propose an understanding of Abramo's achievement that does justice to its complexity.

# I

Mario Pedrosa, an influential Brazilian art critic, offers insightful comments on Abramo's style as a graphic artist. He remarks that in Abramo's woodcuts, "the material is always respected" and that, "Feeling in his hand the weight and predominant direction of each of his tools, Abramo makes use of them with genuine virtuosity" (94). In "Macumba," as in most of his pieces from the 1950s on, the visual texture of the finished print makes the viewer immediately aware of something specific to Abramo's medium—the wood from which the graphic effects are drawn, together with the artist's work with tools on the material.

The woodcut Hayter reproduces cites a few well-known artworks. Its composition, together with the importance of visual rhythm in its organization, bring to mind a landmark work of Modern painting, Matisse's "Dancers." Abramo's print diverges from this model in ways that are immediately apparent. While "Dancers" is an oil painting of monumental scale, "Macumba" is a work on paper that measures only ten-and-a-half by thirteen-and-a-half inches. Once we notice the reference to Matisse, Abramo's print still does not seem the lesser piece, or even a work in a less prestigious medium. Instead of the vibrant color of "Dancers," we find only degrees of black and white—yet these are sufficient to create endless graphic effects, specific to the art of the printer who works on wood. The reference to "Dancers" in *Macumba*, a direct acknowledgment of Abramo's debt to Matisse, opens the way for the Brazilian artist to call attention to the resources of woodcutting.

The title of the print, *Macumba*, emphasizes its figurative dimension, thereby raising a new set of artistic and cultural issues. *Macumba* is the most common word used to designate Afro-Brazilian religion in southern Brazil.[1] The dancers in Abramo's picture will be immediately recognized by Brazilians as women who participate in a *macumba* ceremony and move to the rhythm of Afro-Brazilian percussion, probably in shimmering candlelight.

As indicated, the depiction of Afro-Brazilian culture had been a central concern for Brazilian artists since the 1920s. Abramo's prints belong to the project that led Mario de Andrade to include a chapter also entitled "Macumba" in his experimental narrative, *Macunaíma* (1928), and Tarsila do Amaral, an artist Abramo admired, to paint "A negra" (Abramo, *Depoimentos*). Again, it is productive to note the ways in which Abramo departs from the works he cites.

The attention devoted to Afro-Brazilian culture by the avant-garde Brazilian artists of the 1920s was clearly inspired by the role of primitivism in international Modernism. In a well-known essay by Antonio Candido, we find an authoritative (but also gently ironic) account of this artistic exchange:

> Finally, we know well the role that primitive art, folklore, ethnography had in shaping the aesthetics of Modern art, which has always been very attentive to the archaic and popular elements repressed by Academicism. But in Brazil primitive cultures are a part of daily life, or are live memories of a fairly recent past. The terrible daring of a Picasso, a Brancusi, a Max Jacob, or a Tristan Tzara are, in truth, more coherent with our cultural heritage than with theirs. The familiarity we already had with Black fetishism, with the *calungas* ("fetish"), the *ex-votos* ("votive offerings"), folkloric poetry, all predisposed us to accept and assimilate artistic processes that in Europe corresponded to a deep rupture with the social milieu and mental traditions. Our Modernists absorbed information about European avant-garde art very quickly, educated themselves in psychoanalysis, and shaped a type of expression at once local and universal, finding European influence through submersion in Brazilian detail. (121)[2]

This passage articulates a productive approach to Abramo's *Macumba*; the last sentence in particular may be taken as an apt description of the relationship between Abramo's woodcut and Matisse's famous canvas. At the same time, since Abramo engages in a distinctive way with the issues formulated by Candido, his work calls attention to the difficulties confronted by Brazilian Modernists attempting to represent Afro-Brazilian culture; more interestingly yet, Abramo proposes a new approach to this enduring problem. "Macumba" demonstrates how difficult it is to confidently employ the plural "we" to evoke a culture that encompasses the Modernist artist, Afro-Brazilian religion, the critic and his—or her—readers.

Abramo's woodcut creates an effect of respectful distance vis-à-vis Afro-Brazilian religion and culture. Its composition stresses the space that divides the artist from the scene he recreates and thereby assigns to the viewer a position on the outside as well. At the same time that this detached viewpoint registers the fact that artist and public do not belong among the group depicted, it opens the way for Abramo to construct an image that stresses the integrity of the circle of black women moving together. Due to its near abstract quality, this print all but dissolves the boundaries between one woman and the other, and so presents the *macumba* ceremony as a community ritual. Abramo's exploration of visual rhythm, effective and directly indebted to Matisse as it is, acquires a new connotation in this context: it renders the ceremony's rhythm of movement and percussion in a new medium. Abramo fashions a visual equivalent of this central element of Afro-Brazilian culture and uses it as the key formal principle for his own artwork. "Macumba" is an artist's homage to Afro-Brazilian culture that is enabled precisely by the acknowledged distance between artist and community.

Even as Abramo's solution builds on the solutions of an earlier generation of Brazilian Modernists, it diverges from them in significant ways. His woodcut refers to and, indeed, directly cites a chapter entitled "Macumba" in Mario de Andrade's *Macunaíma*, which describes an Afro-Brazilian ceremony. However, in Mario de Andrade's book, at the end of the ceremony, several intellectuals join the community for a party and "um samba de arromba" ("a terrific samba"). There is an unmistakable contrast between this story of easy intermingling and Abramo's strategy of carefully establishing the distance that separates artist and community. At the same time that Abramo's citation of *Macunaíma* registers his debt to Mario de Andrade, it is slightly colored by irony.

"Macumba" also brings to mind a landmark work of Brazilian Modernism, Tarsila do Amaral's "A Negra" (*The Black Woman*). The composition of Tarsila's "remarkable" oil painting (Dawn Ades, 134) is that of an individual portrait, yet its simplified lines endow the figure with the characteristics of a type at once ethnic and social (Coli). The reserved expression of her half-closed eyes—her "olhar desconfiado" (*mistrustful gaze*) as Fábio Lopes de Souza Santos puts it—stresses the social distance between model and artist. The less than friendly look with which "A Negra" returns the gaze of the observer produces an alienating effect similar to that which Abramo will later create in his woodcut. Tarsila do Amaral's psychological subtlety keeps this portrait from becoming a caricature, despite the exaggerated ethnic features of the figure and the distorted depiction of her body. Yet this approach is certainly risky. A little less sensitivity and tact on the part of the artist and the image she created could have merely reproduced prejudice rather than recontextualizing it. The originality of Abramo's solution is again apparent. Rather than construct a type, his woodcut evokes the image of a community of black women by representing them at the very moment when they engage, together, in a cultural practice from which artist and viewer are excluded.

The print reproduced by Hayter thus presents Abramo as an artist in control of his medium, and engaging in a dialogue with Brazilian and international Modern art. Abramo's approach to the issue of representing Afro-Brazilian culture owes its effectiveness both to his exploration of the tense boundary between figurative and abstract art and to his use of a detached viewpoint. Rather than portray an exotic or primitive religious ceremony, Abramo's "Macumba" portrays a community that the artist admires but to which he does not belong, and does so from a respectful distance.

This strategy of detachment leads to losses as well. Abramo's near-abstract image makes it impossible for the viewer to identify the rhythm to which the dancers in the picture are moving, or indeed what movements they make. For those who practice Afro-Brazilian religion, this information is essential because it indicates which spirits are present. Yet the detached viewpoint itself functions as the sign for such losses: artist and viewers are constructed as outsiders.

Finally—and most interesting of all—Abramo's woodcut directs our attention to the artist's debt to Afro-Brazilian culture. The formal principle upon which he relies to organize this piece—visual rhythm—is abstracted from the rhythm of percussion and movement in *macumba* ceremonies. His contact with Afro-Brazilian culture afforded insight into the artistic possibilities of rhythm. By exploring visual rhythm, he balances figuration and abstraction; at the same time, he depicts Afro-Brazilian culture. Abramo composes a woodcut that may be enjoyed as an abstract piece.

# II

Abramo's interest in Afro-Brazilian ceremonies lasted for a considerable period. The print Hayter reproduces is part of a series of works in various media that share the title *Macumba* (Abramo, *Desenhos; Cento e Trinta e Três Obras*, 111; *Enciclopédia*). In a 1984 foreword to an exhibition of his drawings, Abramo reflects on how much he has learned from observing these ceremonies and offers some interesting remarks on the importance of Afro-Brazilian culture for his artistic development.

Abramo believes that his "fast and synthetic" style of drawing owes much to the experience of attending *macumba* ceremonies:

> For nearly two years I went to *macumba* ceremonies at the *terreiro* of the *mãe de santo* Dona Dalva in Caxias, as a spectator whose interest was purely artistic. Their rhythm and sumptuousness were very important incentives for me to develop a fast type of drawing, which could synthesize that movement that needed to be transformed in lines. (*Desenhos e Gravuras*)

Abramo registers his debt with gratitude and evident admiration. At the same time, he marks his position as that of an outsider and carefully states that his own approach to Afro-Brazilian culture is mediated and, indeed, shaped by art: he is a "spectator whose interest is purely artistic."

Though Abramo's foreword only briefly mentions printing (as seems appropriate in the catalogue of an exhibition of drawings), his passing remarks are interesting. In the 1980s, the curator notes, Abramo was a "consecrated printer." He could assume that the relatively small audience for art shows in São Paulo would be familiar with his prints, and would probably know of the woodcut Hayter reproduces. In this context, Abramo's observation that printing, in contrast to drawing, "requires slower and more careful" work because the artist "may not make mistakes" when carving, serves as an implicit formulation of a formal problem that he addressed in the woodcut discussed earlier. For all the slow and deliberate work a printer is required to perform, "Macumba" evokes rapid movement by exploring visual rhythm, instead of relying on the flowing line of drawing.

Abramo places his interest in *macumba*, and its influence on his art, in the context of his move to Rio de Janeiro, where he lived for two years. His description of Rio stresses the presence of Afro-Brazilian culture. Among the city's "infinite variety of motives," he mentions "the people, the mountains, the bay, the lagoons," but also, pointedly, the *macumbas* and "the beautiful faces of negro women" (*Desenhos e Gravuras*). Finally, Abramo quotes a one-word definition for this phase of his art proposed by his friend Geraldo Ferraz: "negritude."

The second part of this chapter discusses a piece that makes the artist's admiration for the beauty of Afro-Brazilian women especially clear: an illustration for the first edition of Cassiano Ricardo's *Marcha para Oeste*. The numerous contrasts between this piece and the art-work discussed in the first section bring to light a new dimension of Abramo's talent and career. He was not yet a "consecrated printer" at the time that he created this illustration. This was a work produced in response to a specific professional request; it clearly did not aspire to the status of autonomous art. For a considerable time, Abramo earned his living as an illustrator and journalist. These professional activities extended into his political life. Not only was Abramo one of the founders of a journalist's union; he was an activist affiliated ini-tially with the Communist Party and later—after being expelled for refusing to make a caricature of Trotsky—a member of the Socialist Party (Aracy Amaral, 36; Oficina, 46).

Perhaps because the book for which this illustration was made is itself saturated with the politics of the period, the images that Abramo creates allow us to see him at work as a committed artist. A particu-lar piece, which has an Afro-Brazilian woman in the foreground, sheds light on the artwork reproduced by Hayter. Abramo's intelli-gent illustration brings into clear focus concerns that barely surface in *Macumba*. This illustration not only reworks, with insight and irony, a figure of the black woman that is familiar and nearly stereotypical in Brazil; it critically engages with its political instrumentalization during the 1940s.

The book Abramo illustrates, Cassiano Ricardo's *Marcha para Oeste*, articulates a political position diametrically opposed to the artist's. This extended nonfiction prose work—or "sociological essay" as the writer calls it—aims to define the Brazilian nation in order to establish the best way to govern it.[3] Its concluding chapters directly advocate the regime in power, Getúlio Vargas's dictatorial *Estado Novo* (1937–1945). For Ricardo, the Vargas dictatorship corresponds to Brazil's self-recovery (Lenharo, 61). Since Abramo's socialism put him at odds with the dictatorship, to remain true to his views while illustrating Ricardo's book, he had to take chances.

As a result of this unlikely collaboration between a writer and an illustrator identified with antagonistic political camps, in the entire first edition of *Marcha para Oeste* text and illustration are at odds with one another. We find an acute instance of the tension between text and illustration—a tension that, as David Bland articulates, persists throughout the history of illustrated books. In this case, Abramo's eloquent images tell alternative stories that function as ironic counterpoints to Ricardo's heavily ideological tale of how Brazil took shape. The artist's treatment of the Afro-Brazilian woman is a case in point. Abramo pointedly calls attention to this figure, even though it is virtually nonexistent in Ricardo's narrative.

Ricardo's account of the evolution of the Brazilian nation-state rests on an argument about *miscigenação* (racial mixture). The writer's part historical, part mythical tale narrates the expeditions that explored and settled the interior of Brazil in colonial times—the *bandeiras*—as the key moment when the "three races" mingled and, through "love," gave origin to a mixed-race people. It is not surprising to find Ricardo drawing on stereotypes to create his picture of the "three races:"

> In the formation of our biological democracy, the Indian participates with his social mobility, the black with his abundance of feeling and warmth, the Portuguese with his spirit of adventure and command. Three well-defined psychological traits form the moral fabric of the *bandeira*: command, obedience, and movement. While [the *bandeira*] is command, the moment belongs to the *mameluco* (*mestizo* of white and Indian); while it is in movement, the moment belongs to the Indian; when it stops, the moment belongs to the black. (277)

In this passage, Ricardo's treatment of miscegenation establishes both that the *bandeiras* are hierarchical—even as they are mixed—and that the white man holds the position of power.

The anthropologist John Norvell has identified a similarly contradictory structure in the argumentation of classic works of Brazilian social science, some of them contemporaneous with *Marcha para Oeste*. According to Norvell, the following paradox underlies discussions of miscegenation in Brazil:

> The "Brazilian" is, then, a genealogical paradox that, in a linguistic construction, is a mixture, a product of three different races; however, as a grammatical active subject, he mixes with two of these races, but not with the third, the European, because there is, in this instance, an assumed continuity. (257)

Ricardo's contradictory understanding of miscegenation thus partakes in a widespread pattern. However, *Marcha para Oeste* goes beyond simply relying on a familiar cultural construct, superimposing upon it a direct political argument.

The expression "biological democracy" is key to Ricardo's effort to legitimate Getúlio Vargas's *Estado Novo*. In the passage quoted above, this phrase asserts both that the *bandeira* is political and that its hierarchical structure is grounded in nature. In subsequent chapters, *Marcha para Oeste* argues that the Vargas dictatorship is patterned on the *bandeiras*. The *Estado Novo* thus appears as a type of democracy that is "original" to Brazil; as such, Ricardo maintains, it is the only kind of state that is appropriate for the nation. The conventional Brazilian understanding of miscegenation is put to immediate, efficient political use: *Marcha para Oeste* draws on the absolute force of the notion of nature to legitimate the Vargas dictatorship.

Vera Kutzinski's arguments about the ideology of *mestizaje* (racial mixture) and the figure of the *mulata* in Cuba provide insight into both Ricardo's text and Abramo's ironic illustrations. Ricardo's narrative of miscegenation follows a model that, according to Kutzinski, occurs frequently in the literature of the Caribbean and Hispanic America, "most notoriously in Brazil;" Abramo relies on irony to expose the ideological character of that model. For Kutzinski, ideologies of *mestizaje* throughout Latin America correspond to "a peculiar form of multiculturalism" that "acknowledges, indeed celebrates racial diversity, while at the same time disavowing divisive social realities" (5). Capturing the problems inherent in Ricardo's hierarchical understanding of racial mixture, the above passage also provides insight into Abramo's achievement. While Ricardo's rhetoric masks the inequalities implicit in his image of a nation in harmony, Abramo's illustrations draw attention to the "divisive social realities" to which Kutzinski refers.

The artist brings unexpected humor, intelligence, and a light touch to the complex, discouraging, and undoubtedly risky task of illustrating an argument to which he does not subscribe and which serves the interests of the regime in power. Unlike his artistic prints, these illustrations are figurative, direct, and make their point quickly. Even if they have a didactic quality, Abramo's illustrations succeed in critiquing prevailing ideologies without being obvious or moralizing.

An illustration for one of Ricardo's chapters on the *bandeiras* takes the form of a two-frame comic strip: while the left frame faithfully represents the argument of *Marcha para Oeste*, the one on the right undermines it. On the left side, Abramo depicts the *bandeira* as the effort of three races working together. Three men of equal height, one of each race, together look in the same direction. Each has props that specify the role of his "race" in Ricardo's account. The white man wears the hat, vest, and belt that conventionally identify the leader of the expedition, or *bandeirante*; meanwhile, the Afro-Brazilian has a heavy trunk on his head, and the Indian holds a bow. This image of collaborative effort is dismantled in the right frame of the comic strip. This second picture draws our attention to the inequality of power and the threat of violence that constitute the relation between the *bandeirante* and his African slave. In the foreground, two black men are engaged in demanding physical labor; in the background, a white man with the hat of a *bandeirante* and a weapon at his waist calmly oversees their work. By stressing that the African slave works under coercion, Abramo undermines the illusion of racial harmony projected by Ricardo's tale. This illustration also represents the African as a worker, a prevalent figure in the committed art of the period. Abramo thus succeeds in opening a space for socialist perspective even within the massively hierarchical conception of Brazil advocated in *Marcha para Oeste*.

Abramo introduces another missing character—that of the Afro-Brazilian woman—in a striking illustration placed at the end of a chapter on *bandeiras* and miscegenation. In the preceding pages, Ricardo has turned to the systematic coercion in the *bandeira* that led to sexual encounters between men and women of different "races." After specifying that "the crossing (*a cruza*) of Indians and blacks was brought about by the priest and the slaveowning *bandeirante*," Ricardo proceeds sentimentally:

> [This process] substituted violence through the cleverness of the *bandeirante* and the complicity of the priest, and contributed lovingly to the miscegenation [of Indian and black], thus far regarded as impossible, given the mutual repulsion between blacks and Indians. (290)

Following an all too familiar ideological pattern, this passage denies the violence of such sexual encounters. By contrast, Abramo's illustration tells the story of a forced embrace that is neither loving nor happy.

At the center of his illustration, an Indian man and an attractive, African-looking woman hold one another; they are flanked by a priest and a *bandeirante* who appear to be pushing them together. The woman's nude torso occupies most of the foreground. The couple does not have much room in which to move and they look past one another with impassive expressions. Abramo's use of distortion heightens the oppressive atmosphere of the scene. The hands of the four figures, depicted in the foreground, are disproportionately large and seem to form a tight circle around the couple. Raised in benediction, the priest's hand looks remarkably like a claw.

Abramo's image diverges most from Ricardo's narrative in his treatment of the Afro-Brazilian woman. Though Ricardo's stress on miscegenation requires him to address women, he refers to them only briefly—and white women, pointedly, play no role in the creation of a *mestizo* race. Moreover, though Indian and black women take part in the process of miscegenation, they are barely human; to quote one of the author's memorable articulations, women are "live points of mediation which one race uses to fuse with another" (293). Once again, Kutinzki's comments about the role of the *mulata* in the ideology of Cuban nationalism provide insight:

> The mulata may be the signifier of Cuba's unity-in-racial-diversity, but she has no part in it. For the *mestizo* nation is a male homosocial construct premised precisely upon the disappearance of the feminine. (165)

The points of convergence (and divergence) between Cuban constructions of the nation and the images projected by *Marcha para Oeste* are evident. Ricardo's Brazil, like Cuba, is imagined as a homosocial community; the Indian and black women of his story, like the Cuban *mulata*, are essential to the *mestizo* nation even as that nation is premised upon their disappearance. However, Abramo brings the figure elided by Ricardo's text to the foreground, calling into question the imagined harmony of the Brazilian nation.

Abramo transforms Ricardo's romantic tale into a story of violence. Again, the artist's work is distinguished by careful technique and considerable empathy. Through the diagonal lines implicit in the composition, Abramo directs the viewer's attention to the attractive, very dark, uncovered, and African-looking female figure in the right foreground. Strong, well-balanced contrasts between black, white, and two lighter shades contribute to making the female figure the center of attention. A lone woman surrounded by three men and touched by two of them, she is clearly overpowered. Though she returns the touch of the Indian man, the Afro-Brazilian woman neither smiles nor meets his eyes; instead she looks to the horizon beyond the figures surrounding her. Abramo's composition calls attention to the inequality of power and the threat of force underlying the sexual encounters Ricardo imagines as idyllic. At the same time, through his empathetic depiction, the artist stresses the psychological conflict and pain that the Afro-Brazilian woman experiences.

Her action—she does return the touch of the Indian man—appears as a reasonable choice: what else could she have done?

In the upper portion of the illustration we reencounter Abramo's sense of humor and his habit of citation. A grotesque and vaguely obscene papaya tree appears to sprout from the head of the Indian man; next to it—and almost as big as the tree—there is a sketch of a human figure that is possibly the couple's *mestizo* offspring. A river seems to run from the priest's hair, around the tree and into the mountains in the distance. In the context of Ricardo's enthusiastic—indeed, gushing—descriptions of "the paradisiacal happiness of cross-breeding in the midst of the wilderness," this scene may be taken as Abramo's parody of the tropical paradise, including a new version of the tree of life and a poorly formed, disproportionately tall Brazilian Adam.

At the same time, the scene in the upper part of the illustration includes an unmistakable reference to an oil painting by Tarsila do Amaral, "O Mamoeiro" (*The Papaya Tree*). Certain of the figures included here appear in her canvas: children, a river, and a very tall papaya tree. However, whereas Tarsila's canvas is, to quote Ades again, "full of life" (134) and paints a nearly idyllic (if avant-gardist) image of small-town life in rural Brazil, when Abramo reworks the same motifs the result is disquieting. Tarsila's papaya tree is stylized and whimsical, presiding over a colorful scene; Abramo's grotesque tree seems out of place, hovering above the unhappy embracing couple. Again, Abramo's irony is unmistakable, if subtle.

For all Abramo's effective undermining of Ricardo's hierarchical views on the nation, his own treatment of the Afro-Brazilian woman nonetheless participates in Brazil's racialized culture. The artist works with a conventional image of the black woman as exotic and sexually attractive, which is undeniably marked by prejudice. (In this respect, Abramo's figure is similar to that of the *mulata*, whose functions in the history of Brazilian literature Teófilo de Queiroz has examined in detail.) It is significant that the illustration I have been discussing appeared in a commercial book, directed to a fairly broad audience. In art books, one encounters various drawings of nude women by Abramo that do not fit the paradigm of exoticism; the open acknowledgment of sexuality in these drawings is often in fact moving (*Cento e Trinta e Três Obras*, 37, 59, 66, 68, 73). It is nevertheless difficult to imagine that in Brazil of the 1940s an explicit treatment of the nude torso of a white woman would find its way into print. Clearly, then, even as this illustration directs our attention to a history of violence against Afro-Brazilian women, it does so by putting into circulation an image that bears the marks of that violence and continues to perform it.

At this point, it is helpful to remember Judith Butler's argument concerning injurious speech. For Butler, efforts to control injurious speech partake in a dogmatism that is itself both intellectually and politically damaging:

> Whether it is the censorship of particular kinds of representation or the circumscription of the domain of public discourse itself, the effort to tighten the reins on speech undercuts those political efforts to exploit speech itself for its insurrectionary effects. (162)

Butler's formulation enables us to view Abramo's achievement in *Marcha para Oeste* in the most general terms yet. The dramatic power of this illustration resides precisely in the artist's redeployment of a familiar image. The more aware we are of the touching youth and attractiveness of the Afro-Brazilian woman in the foreground, the more painfully aware we become of the extent to which they make her vulnerable to exploitation.

*   *   *

This chapter has explored Lívio Abramo's engagement with Afro-Brazilian culture by discussing two works of a very different nature. The woodcut, "Macumba," reveals an artist who is concerned with exploring the tensions between abstraction and figuration, and with conducting a complex dialogue with various currents of Modern art both in Brazil and internationally. Working with visual rhythm, Abramo succeeds at once in representing an Afro-Brazilian ceremony and in creating a work of art that may be enjoyed on an abstract level. By contrast, the illustrations for *Marcha para Oeste* are effective examples of committed art. Unambiguously figurative and direct, they show Abramo relying on humor and irony to resist the hegemonic thrust of ideologies of hierarchical nationalism. Of particular interest is the dramatic illustration that not only brings into focus the historical violence suffered by Afro-Brazilian women but also calls attention to their courage and resilience.

The central assumption of this chapter is that it is productive to discuss these two types of work in tandem. An examination of Abramo's illustrations brings elements to light that are consistently pushed into the background of his artwork: both the political implications and the sexual overtones of his interest in Afro-Brazilian culture. (Of course, the discussion of Abramo's illustrations also sheds light on the conflicted cultural and political life of Brazil during the

Vargas dictatorship.) Abramo's woodcut, on the other hand, shows how much he learned, as an artist, from his contact with Afro-Brazilian culture. Observing the *macumba* ceremonies, Abramo gains insight into the place of rhythm that enables him to negotiate the tensions between abstract and figurative approaches.

Abramo's committed illustrations and his artwork are both rewarding objects of discussion. The artist seems to move with ease from one type of work to the other and to excel at both. Abramo deserves to have the last word here on the issue of commitment and autonomy in art. He worked long and hard to have printing accepted in Brazil as an "autonomous art" and no longer simply as "an aid to illustration" (*Oficina*, 88 and 46). Though he was often very critical of committed art, he never dismissed commitment as a failed project:

> Käthe Kollwitz' prints are extraordinary, although they are simply protest prints; they are good from an artistic viewpoint. And that is why all Russian painting after Stalin is worth nothing. It is purely formalistic; it focuses on events in the Soviet Union, the workers' labor, but in an academic way, lifelessly. Any pre-Stalinist painting, no matter how abstract, is worth much more than the painting of the later period. (*Oficina*, 47)

## Notes

* Earlier versions of this chapter were read at the meetings of the American Comparative Literature Association (San Juan, Puerto Rico, April 2002) and the Associação Brasileira de Literatura Comparada (Belo Horizonte, Brazil, July 2002), in a lecture series at Binghamton University, to the students of the Master's in History at the Universidade Federal de Minas Gerais (Brazil), and to the Centro de Estudos Comparativos and the Program in Comparative Literature at the Universidade de Lisboa. I would like to thank Carmen Ferradás and Hilton Silva; Júnia Furtado; Helena Buescu and João Ferreira Duarte for invitations that afforded me rewarding opportunities for dialogue. My audience on these occasions helped me develop my arguments with questions and insightful comments. Dale Tomich contributed his reading skills (and more) to this chapter. I would like to thank Alexandra Isfahani-Hammond for the invitation that started me on the road to writing it and especially for her patience, and grace, *na hora da onça beber água*. Another very special thank you to Alcione Abramo, who was generous with information and support; Bia Abramo, Hélio Guimarães, César Braga-Pinto, and Rachelle Moore were very helpful in many ways.

1. *Candomblé*, another word that refers to Afro-Brazilian religion, is most commonly used in Bahia (and the north of the country) and in

the United States as well. However, the differences between *macumba* and *candomblé* are not simply a matter of regional usage. Roger Bastide, in his authoritative *The African Religion of Brazil*, notes, "in addition to the Yoruba 'nations' [ . . . ] there were Bantu 'nations' whose ceremonies were known as *macumba*" (205).

2. There are suggestive points of contact (and contrast) between Candido's argument and that of another fundamental Latin American text of the mid-century, the famous prologue to *El reino de este mundo*, in which Alejo Carpentier lays out his conception of *lo real maravilloso*. Carpentier, too, inverts commonplace assumptions about the relation between the European avant-grade and Latin America and referes pointedly to the culture of Afro-America. However, Carpentier's irony is by far more apparent than Candido's. These parallels deserve a lengthy quotation:

> This [contrast] became particularly clear to me during my stay in Haiti, when I found myself in daily contact with something that we may want to call <u>lo real-maravilloso</u>. [ . . . ] There I encountered <u>lo real-maravilloso</u> at each step of the way. But I also thought that the presence and actuality of <u>lo real-maravilloso</u> was not a unique privilege of Haiti, but rather a patrimony of America as a whole, where an inventory of cosmogonies, for example, has not fully been established yet. [ . . . ] Looking at the question from another angle, we'll see that, whereas in Europe folkloric dances, for example, have lost all their magical character and all their power of invocation, in America it is difficult to find collective dances that do not have a deep ritual meaning [ . . . ] (16)

Significantly, Carpentier's examples of magical dances include the Cuban *santería* and "the prodigious Negroid version of the feast of Corpus" in Venezuela.

3. This discussion of *Marcha para Oeste* summarizes the second chapter of my *Meninos, Poetas e Heróis*.

## WORKS CITED

Abramo, Lélia. *Vida e arte: Memórias de Lélia Abramo*. São Paulo: Fundação Perseu Abramo, 1997.

Abramo, Lívio. *Brasil-Paraguai*. São Paulo: Memorial da América Latina, 1994.

———. *Cento e Trinta e Três Obras Restauradas*. Asunción, Paraguay: Embajada de Brasil and Centro de Artes Visuales/Museo del Barro, 2001.

———. "Depoimentos." *Enciclopédia de Artes Visuais*. 2003. *Itaúcultural*. December 14, 2003.

———. *Desenhos e Gravuras de 1926 a 1970.* São Paulo: Museu de Arte Moderna, 1972.

———. *Macumba.* 1957. *About Prints.* By S.W. Hayter. London: Oxford University Press, 1962. *Gravura.* 1 May 2004. http://www.gravura.art.br/expo.htm.

———. *Registros de um Percurso.* São Paulo: Museu de Arte Moderna de São Paulo, 1984.

Ades, Dawn. *Art in Latin America: The Modern Era, 1820–1980.* New Haven: Yale University Press, 1989.

Amaral, Aracy. *Arte Para Qué? A Preocupação Social na Arte Brasileira.* São Paulo: Nobel, 1984.

Amaral, Tarsila do. "O Mamoeiro." 1925. São Paulo: Instituto de Estudos Brasileiros. *Coleção Mário de Andrade: Artes Plásticas.* São Paulo: Instituto de Estudos Brasileiros, 1998. By Marta Rossetti Batista and Yone Soares de Lima. Figure 25. *Tarsila do Amaral Site.* May 1, 2004. http://www.tarsiladoamaral.com.br/images/JPG/omamoeiro50.jpg.

———. "A negra." 1923. São Paulo: Museu de Arte Contemporânea. *Art in Latin America: The Modern Era, 1820–1980.* By Dawn Ades. New Haven: Yale University Press, 1989. Figure 6.14. *Museu de Arte Contemporânea de São Paulo.* May 1, 2004. http://www.mac.usp.br/exposicoes/02/semana22/colecao/tarsila/ANegra.html.

Andrade, Mario de. *Macunaíma: O Herói Sem Nenhum Caráter.* Ed. Telê Porto Ancona Lopes. Paris: Archives; Brasília, Braz: CNPq, 1988.

Batista, Marta Rossetti and Yone Soares de Lima. *Coleção Mário de Andrade: Artes Plásticas.* São Paulo: Instituto de Estudos Brasileiros, 1998.

Bastide, Roger. *The African Religions of Brazil: Toward a Sociology of the Interpenetration of Civilizations.* Baltimore: Johns Hopkins, 1978.

Bland, David. *A History of Book Illustration: The Illuminated Manuscript and the Printed Book.* London: Faber and Faber, 1958.

Butler, Judith. *Excitable Speech: A Politics of the Performative.* New York: Routledge, 1997.

Candido, Antonio. *Literatura e Sociedade.* São Paulo: Companhia Editora Nacional, 1980.

Carpentier, Alejo. *El Reino de Este Mundo.* México: Siglo Veintiuno, 1983.

Chiarelli, Tadeu. "Matrizes do Expressionismo no Brasil." *Enciclopédia de Artes Visuais.* 2003. *Itaúcultural.* December 14, 2003.

Coli, Jorge. "Conceitualismo." *O Contexto.* São Paulo: Museu de Arte Contemporânea, 2000. May 1, 2004.

*Enciclopédia de Artes Visuais.* 2003. *Itaúcultural.* December 14, 2003. http://www.itaucultural.org.br/Aplic Externas/Enciclopedia/artesvisvais 2003/i.

Escobar, Ticio. "La Lección Restaurada." *Cento e Trinta e Três Obras Restauradas.* By Lívio Abramo. Asunción, Paraguay: Embajada de Brasil and Centro de Artes Visuales/Museo del Barro, 2001. 31–47.

Ferraz, Geraldo. [Introduction]. *Desenhos e Gravuras de 1926 a 1970.* By Lívio Abramo. São Paulo: Museu de Arte Moderna, 1972.

Hayter, S.W. *About Prints*. London: Oxford University Press, 1962.

Kutzinski, Vera. *Sugar's Secrets: Race and the Erotics of Cuban Nationalism*. Charlottesville: University Press of Virginia, 1993.

Lenharo, Alcir. *Sacralização da Política*. Campinas, Brazil: Papirus and Editora da UNICAMP, 1986.

"Lívio Abramo." *Enciclopédia de Artes Visuais*. 2003. *Itaúcultural*. December 14, 2003. http://www.itaucultural.org.br/AplicExternas/ Enciclopedia/artesvisuais2003/index.cfm?fuseaction = Detalhe&CD_ Verbete = 3935.

Morais, Frederico. *Destaques Hilton de Gravura*. Rio de Janeiro: Companhia Souza Cruz, 1982.

Moreira, Luiza Franco. *Meninos, Poetas e Heróis: Aspectos de Cassiano Ricardo do Modernismo ao Estado Novo*. São Paulo: EDUSP, 2001.

Norvell, John M. "A Brancura Desconfortável das Camadas Médias Brasileiras." *Raça Como Retórica: A Construção da Diferença*. Rio de Janeiro: Civilização Brasileira, 2001. 245–267.

Oficina de Gravura SESC Tijuca. *Gravura Brasileira Hoje: Depoimentos*. Vol. 3. Rio de Janeiro: Oficina de Gravura SESC Tijuca, 1997.

Ricardo, Cassiano. *Marcha para Oeste: A Influência da Bandeira na Formação Social e Política do Brasil*. Illustrations by Lívio Abramo. Rio de Janeiro: José Olympio, 1940.

Santos, Fabio Lopes de Souza. "A Pintura Antropofágica de Tarsila do Amaral." Unpublished essay, 2002.

Queiroz Júnior, Teófilo de. *Preconceito de Cor e a Mulata na Literatura Brasileira*. São Paulo: Ática, 1982.

# CHAPTER 10

# Blood, Memory, and Nation: Massacre and Mourning in Edwidge Danticat's *The Farming of Bones*

### Shreerekha Subramanian

Ours is a century marked by massacre. There is a tendency to let history swallow massacres whole or allow only "legitimate" portions to be seen by posterity. I am interested in uncovering the erased populations caught in the tentacles of disremembering. I raise the question of Haiti, its awe-inspiring blackness, and a massacre that clouded its historical imagination for the entire century just passed. Excavating the detritus of history, I am curious about what is left, the materials with which a ravaged people navigate their current course. Theories of history, mourning, and memory proposed by Lois Parkinson Zamora, Deborah Cohn, and George Handley provide critical apparatus for this study.

> In 1937, without a qualm, *El Jefe* had ordered the slaughter of some twenty thousand black Haitians. Killing, he had decided, was the easiest, cheapest and most efficient method of removing the blacks who squatted on Dominican territory or toiled as sugar cutters in its large plantations. A Negrophobe, Trujillo disguised the fact that he had Negro blood in his own veins. Even the dusky tinge to his complexion was lightened with makeup. He ignored the fact that most Dominicans were, like himself, of mixed blood or Negro, and declared his nation officially white. (Diederich, 12)

Bernard Diederich writes with journalistic precision of the leader known more familiarly as the "goat." President Rafael Trujillo, a leader

Hitlerian in kinship, unable to see his own body in relation to the history he writes upon the back of his people, declares his nation, the Dominican Republic, to be white. In order to keep it so, he decides to reduce the blight of blackness by eliminating as many blacks as possible, mostly Haitian workers and the darker Dominicans. Historians still argue about the numbers slaughtered, driven mad, disappeared, and drowned. Somewhere between 5,000 and 30,000, the numbers swim in the murky forced erasure that Trujillo necessarily kept vague. Haiti, winning independence in 1804, became a marker of black nationalism, the nemesis of European nations and ruling classes. It posed a particular threat to the elites of the Dominican Republic. Ernesto Sagás describes the repellent *antihaitianismo* that took root there:

> As the product of a bloody slave insurrection and racial strife, the independence of Haiti in 1804 represented a terrifying prospect for white nations: the massacre of most whites, the destruction of European civilization, and their replacement by a black republic led by the ex-slaves themselves. Even the newly independent Latin American nations turned their backs on Haiti and excluded it from hemispheric deliberations, such as the 1826 Congress of Panama. In spite of its human achievements, in the minds of white elites the Haitian Revolution became synonymous with chaos, violence, and black savagery. If the Haitian Revolution provoked feelings of rejection by elites in the rest of the hemisphere, for the Dominican elites, neighboring Haiti was their gravest concern. Antihaitianismo ideology thus provided Dominicans with a convenient shield of cultural superiority vis-à-vis an ostracized nation. As contradictory as it may seem, and as a result of antihaitianismo ideology, even the lowest, poorest, and darkest Dominicans are prone to claim cultural—and even racial—superiority over the Haitian people. (Sagás, 4–5)

Haunting questions arise from such seismic quakes. How do a people remember their ancestors and cherished stories in a world that disremembers their history and claims that it never happened? How do those who have their lives, loves, and nation wrenched from them exercise their humanity and world citizenship? In Haiti, whose blackness casts the pall of invisibility upon its people and causes demagogues, hegemons, and Haiti's own hemispheric cousins to shroud such stories, the true desperation of Haitian survival emerges. Such a condition fosters the emergence of a community with the dead.

In *The Farming of Bones* (1998), Edwidge Danticat spins a love story between two Haitian workers, Amabelle Désir and Sebastien

Onius, caught on the wrong side of the island in the cutting winds of 1937. Danticat's authorial inspiration for this text resides at the site of death itself, a space that swallows memory:

> It wasn't until Danticat stood on the banks of the River Massacre itself, where the killings had taken place, that she fully realized that she wanted to make a novel out of the story. (The river is named after another 19th century genocidal episode that had occurred on its banks.) "It was really strange to stand there—it was low tide, and people were bathing, and washing their clothes in the water," recalls Danticat. "There were no markers. I felt like I was standing on top of a huge mass grave, and just couldn't see the bodies. That's the first time I remember thinking, 'Nature has no memory'—a line that later made its way into the book—and that's why we have to have memory".
> (*Publisher's Weekly*, 43)

Danticat's immersion in the imagined lives of her characters evokes Walter Benjamin's triadic bleeding between storyteller, history, memory, and audience. Like Benjamin's Nikolai Leskov, Danticat speaks not only to a Haitian audience, both within the nation's borders and in the diaspora, but also to citizens and noncitizens of other nation-states, given the dialogical condition of the community generated by the literary writer (Zamora, 174). Danticat upon the river, resonant with the last scene of her novel where Amabelle ponders the river's deceptive calm, recalls the spirit of Benjamin's authentic storyteller. What drives the narrative forward and keeps Amabelle moving is her link with the dead: her parents, Antoine Désir and Irelle Pradelle, and her love, Sebastien Onius. In this imagined community, the massacre's survivor finds her humanity, her connection to a fleshy past and her desire to write the rest. Remembering is a political exercise, and not letting go of the dead is an act of love. To live in a world peopled by the dead means that dying itself is a rebirth. This condition, so discordant with Enlightenment epistemologies, is possible only in the aftermath of such a massacre. Fraternity with the dead becomes an exercise in liberty, an effort toward equality between those who live a death in life and those who attain life in death.

This essay rests in an anxious space between Edouard Glissant's forced poetics and Walter Benjamin's conceptualization of history and redemption. Lois Parkinson Zamora's discussion of the "usable past," of a history kindled alive by storytelling, provides further foundation. As theories are borrowed, I heed Edward Said's caution that critical readings must be weighted with historic and geographic specificity in order to recognize their inherent resistance. A theory of Haitians trapped in massacres—like any theory stemming from genocide—needs to remember the genocide itself, not just the idea:

> To measure the distance between theory then and now, there and here, to record the encounter of theory with resistances to it, to move skeptically in the broader political world where such things as the humanities or the great classics ought to be seen as small provinces of the human venture, to map the territory covered by all the techniques of dissemination, communication, and interpretation, to preserve some modest (perhaps shrinking) belief in noncoercive human community: if these are not imperatives, they do at least seem to be attractive alternatives. And what is critical consciousness at bottom if not an unstoppable predilection for alternatives? (Said, 247)

Amabelle provides the alternatives. Through her, we begin to trace a living community with the dead.

My essay is divided into five sections. In the first, I outline Amabelle's invocation of Sebastien Onius. In the second, I consider Amabelle's memories of her parents' drowning. The third section traces Amabelle's precarious link with the living—with Señora Valencia, Juana, Luis, Papi, Kongo, and even Yves, her lifelong mate. The fourth looks at Amabelle's comfort in the arms of women who know death well—Man Rapadou, Man Denise, and even her own mother, Irelle Pradelle. Finally, I arrive at the scene where she lies down at River Massacre on the anniversary of the cutting of 1937: a gesture of good-bye and hello, Amabelle floats comfortably as if returned to the womb, delivering herself into " . . . Sebastien's cave, my father's laughter, my mother's eternity" (414).

In the opening of *The Farming of Bones*, Amabelle Désir and Sebastien Onius make love by the light of the castor oil lamp in her small shack. He promises to take her to the cave across the river, to the place that took their parents from them, the place that returns to them in their dreams. Sebastien retreats to the darkest corner of the room as Amabelle strips so that he may tutor her in seeing the unseen: "It is good for you to learn and trust that I am near you even when you can't place the balls of your eyes on me" (9). From this point on, we become aware that the two are never alone, for the ghosts of their memories take visceral space. When Amabelle says that her lover guards her from the shadows, that he sometimes becomes the shadows themselves, her ambivalent verb usage makes it unclear whether she refers to the living Sebastien or to the ghost of Sebastien who lingers close by, protecting her and guiding her toward the shadows that mark her own ending and birthing.

Amabelle insists upon naming her lover, the cane worker who was murdered as part of an invisible, anonymous blackness, a mass of workers whose own masters hardly knew their names. She repeatedly tells us, "His name is Sebastien Onius," as if his institutional erasure demands this incantation, a talisman both against and into the shadows. These shadows, glimpses into the world of the dead, mirror the color of Amabelle's black skin, the blighted blackness that is the indictment behind Trujillo's second mass slaughter at River Massacre.

When Amabelle is in her room, she remembers Sebastien's advice to lie naked and alone as the day she emerged from the womb. Thinking about the sweat that gathers between her back and the floor, she hopes little water will remain in her body with which to cry, to mourn the losses she accrues with each passing day. In this moment of bereavement that haunts Amabelle throughout the text, she forms a community with the sweat that puddles under the weight of her body, knowing that the answers she seeks are to be found in water. The gesture of reclining in this manner resembles her final act of lying down on River Massacre, a burial ground where there is neither burial nor ground. The river swallows lives incompletely, rising at whim and consuming sojourners like Amabelle's parents. It is the silent repository of those hacked upon its banks, or drowned while crossing it. The river—along with rain, tears, and blood—is a liquid crossing to the other side. Some succeed in crossing over to the neighboring nation, while others remove to the next world.

When Amabelle plans her departure, she sees no farther than River Massacre, where Sebastien promises to meet her. After his disappearance in Trujillo's bloodbath, Amabelle dreams that Sebastien is a resident shadow in the waterfall cave, his ghost mingling with the succor of falling water, and prays that his last fall was broken by this water. She conjures his spirit to comfort her in her death in life. It is significant that Sebastien's mother names him for a saint who dies twice; St. Sebastien returns to his assailants to demonstrate the power of love only to be stoned to death a second time. The paucity of life and the richness of death assume direct proportion.

If we replace "hymen" by "marriage" or "crime," "identity" or "difference," etc., the effect would be the same, the only loss being a certain economic condensation or accumulation, which has not gone unnoticed. It is the "between," whether it names fusion or separation, that thus carries all the force of the operation. The hymen must be determined by the *entre* and not the other way around. The hymen in the text (crime, sexual act, incest, suicide, simulacrum) is inscribed at the very tip of this indecision. This tip advances according to the irreducible excess of the syntactic over the semantic. The word "between" has no full meaning of its own = an incomplete signification. (Derrida, 220–221)

If we deconstruct *The Farming of Bones* using a Derridean tearing of the hymen, we can name the hymen "massacre" or "crime" or "difference," all the while conserving the pathos of the "between." In Derrida's discussion of the incomplete signification of *entre*, inscribing in it the indecision of the excess of the syntactic over the semantic, we return to River Massacre where Amabelle's family attempts to cross back over to Haiti at the height of flood season. Antoine Désir and Irelle Pradelle disappear into the sudden swell of a tide with their arms raised. They leave behind a curious gesture to their muted daughter watching from the shores, waiting for their return—a farewell, a victory sign, a defeat, another signal in the secret language of melancholia.

Is their departure a fusion or a separation? To answer this question, I return to the collectivity with the dead. Though drawn away from the water by the river rats and Don Ignacio, Amabelle never leaves her parents. She communes with them long after their death. River Massacre, symbolic of the *entre*, marks neither fusion nor separation, but the path between life and death, consciousness and dream, child and parent, voiced and voiceless, history and fantasy. Mother and father rest in the *entre*, leaving behind a daughter who learns to heal, birth, and find contentment, and who ultimately loses her life in the same waters that took theirs.

Watching her parents drown, Amabelle plunges into the river so as not to be separated from them. Though she is saved, she meets her parents in dreams and waking fantasies. Amabelle hears her parents calling out to her in Creole; she meets them in a place impossible to navigate in rational discourse, or in Spanish. In the dust storms that cloud the valley, Amabelle makes out a mass of human beings. She sees people walking around her while she is a little girl holding her parents hands, and upon the clearing of the storm, she is led forward by hands extended upward, as if in prayer, as if in union with the ethereal. When Señora Valencia paints and varnishes the baby coffin for little Rafi, Amabelle envies the dead baby who at least has a final bed. Her parents, swallowed by a wave, jolt eternally on the crests and nadirs of their daughter's watery memory.

After making the long journey home to Haiti, after being publicly flogged and loosing most of her travel companions, Amabelle wakes up in a makeshift hospital where her only respite is a sleep that feels like death. Memories of her mother feature a smiling Irelle

Pradelle dressed in glass, assuring her daughter that she will not be alone:

> Your mother was never as far from you as you supposed. You were like my shadow. Always fled when I came to you and only followed when I left you alone. You will be well again, ma belle, Amabelle. I know this to be true. And how can you have ever doubted my love? You, my eternity? (279)

This assurance, this community with dead kin, inspires Amabelle to live. Irelle Pradelle calls her daughter "my eternity," erasing the linear function of time and placing its agency in the hands of those whose time has been wrenched from them. When as an elderly woman Amabelle lies on the river's womb, she imagines she will be carried "into Sebastien's cave, my father's laughter, my mother's eternity" (414). It is now she who calls her mother "eternity," as if it were her mother's possession, as if time were pliable to the demands of a broken heart. Time becomes an ally in this landscape where death mingles with life, sometimes to erase it, sometimes to shout a greeting. For those willing to invite and imagine a community with the dead, time is indeed negotiable.

In the blackness of night when Amabelle imagines that the silent river does not exist, that everyone swallowed in its undertow actually died peacefully, she recalls her mother's death. She remembers how her drowning parents desperately tried to deliver a final message to her. In her mother's raised arm—asking her daughter to jump in or to move farther away?—lies the conundrum that remains unanswered even as Amabelle ascends to her watery grave, or womb. Edouard Glissant illuminates this shifting signifier in Amabelle's life:

> Forced poetics exist where a need for expression confronts an inability to achieve expression. It can happen that this confrontation is fixed in an opposition between the content to be expressed and the language suggested or imposed . . . A forced poetics is created from the awareness of the opposition between a language that one uses and a form of expression that one needs. (Glissant, 120–121)

The condition of the Haitian in the Dominican Republic is a forced poetics, for the eddies of history lie in the difference between Creole and Spanish, between a child's wounded silence and her ability to decipher what is said. Amabelle requires a more lucid language to understand Irelle Pradelle's warning, and finds that language in her final repose at River Massacre. Hers is not the pathological death instinct

Freud elucidates but a will to surpass the limited language of life and become more fluent after death.

> In other words, our image of happiness is indissolubly bound up with the image of redemption. The same applies to our view of the past, which is the concern of history. The past carries with it a temporal index by which it is referred to redemption. There is a secret agreement between past generations and the present one. Our coming was expected on earth. Like every generation that preceded us, we have been endowed with a weak Messianic power, a power to which the past has a claim. That claim cannot be settled cheaply. Historical materialists are aware of that. (Benjamin, 254)

Even for those like Sebastien's father who died in the hurricane, or Amabelle's parents who drowned in the flood, death marks the specific desperation of Haitian workers who cross borders and illegally enter forbidden territories to survive. When even the little boys who ferry wayfarers on their backs refuse to cross the river, Amabelle's parents insist upon doing so because they fear staying on in Dajabon as marked "others." George Handley's reading of family history as "a thematic and structural sine qua non" of post-slavery narrative (Handley, 3) responds to the return of Amabelle's repressed lineage in spite of the violence of the Haitian plantocracy and the pro-Trujillo nationalists. The image of the daughter waiting for her father's return so he can carry her across the River Massacre speaks also to Benjamin's notion of history. Amabelle's happiness is indissolubly bound up with the image of redemption, of the river retreating to reveal her parents, the bullet returning to a place of stasis before consuming Sebastien and his sister's life.

Amabelle is endowed with an almost messianic power upon watching those closest to her die. It is this power that brings her back for a final look at the living with whom she shared her childhood, at Señora Valencia and her kingdom across the border in the Dominican Republic, and then to the river itself which marks her crossing to the next world.

> Mourning is regularly the reaction to the loss of a loved person, or to the loss of some abstraction which has taken the place of one, such as one's country, liberty, an ideal, and so on. In some people the same influences produce melancholia instead of mourning and we consequently suspect them of a pathological disposition. . . . The melancholic displays something else besides which is lacking in mourning—an extraordinary diminution in his self-regard, an impoverishment of his

ego on a grand scale. In mourning it is the world which has become poor and empty; in melancholia it is the ego itself. (Freud, 243, 246)

Freud's binary definition of normative and pathological responses to loss fails to account for the fact that melancholia is the normative condition of oppressed dark "others" trying to survive in the face of an obliterating will toward whiteness. Amabelle's link to the dead delivers hope; it brings Benjamin's indissoluble happiness in the face of a cruel history. It is charged with political power, in the exercise of Amabelle's refusal to let go of that which was wrenched away. In this dire alchemy of class and racial hierarchies, the servant is obliterated from the master's narrative. Amabelle's rejoinder to this omission is her unwillingness to forget, a gesture that is illuminated by George Handley's reading of Derek Walcott's poetics: " . . . slavery is never really behind us, not only because similar conditions may exist in the present, but because it provides the strangely fertile soil from which a wide array of unpredictable, beautiful cultural forms emerge" (Handley, 14).

> Of Señor Pico and the nation that emerges from Trujillo's nationalism, Sagás writes: The Dominican Republic is a good case study of the deliberate manipulation of racial prejudice and nationalism by elites bent on promoting their own definition of nationhood and on maintaining their hold on political and economic power . . . *antihaitianismo* has its origins in the racial prejudices of Spanish colonial society in Santo Domingo. Even before there was a Haiti, the roots of *antihaitianismo* ideology had been planted by the Spanish. (18)

When Señor Pico teaches his wife to shoot a rifle, and she nearly shoots a scampering Amabelle, he is not concerned. After all, his work at the border consists in eliminating the same people who clean, cook, garden, and care for his home and family. More noteworthy is the fact that Amabelle is not surprised by this accident. Shuddering, she remarks, "The señora's strong. She's a good markswoman" (182). Amabelle's depressive condition is bound to the political reality of the nation-space she inhabits. It is a detachment as necessary as her instinct to dodge the flying piece of metal. Despite the fact that the only family Amabelle knows is that of her mistress, that she has spent more of her waking life under her awning than with her parents, her link to this "family" is tenuous. She occupies the space of her body and performs with dexterity and grace. She heals, births, is nearly run over by armored tanks and escapes a whizzing bullet, all because her body exists in the temporal locale of Alegría. Yet her soul, her desire, her dreams flit far away to a place on the riverside called "redemption" where time becomes irrelevant.

Amabelle is distant even from Yves, her companion on the dangerous trek to the border and into Haiti, the provider who extends his home to her. Fanon's prophetic words describe the relationship forged between these two fugitives who remain shrouded in silence: "A national culture under colonial domination is a contested culture whose destruction is sought in systematic fashion. It very quickly becomes a culture condemned to secrecy" (237). They make love once only, to demonstrate that pleasure is still possible after all the barbarity. For twenty-four years, they share the same courtyard without exchanging many words. Their link is an oath of secrecy, a great betrayal. For Amabelle, living is the sin, living that takes its daily toll in the silence between herself and Yves, the sole survivors of their treacherous journey. Unable to love one another and to write a new story, Amabelle waits for the death of President Trujillo to return for a final time to the denizens of her home in Alegría. Long before the twilight of her life, resting in Sebastien's arms, he explains to her that they must travel far to meet because they are *vwayajè*, wayfarers.

> The Messiah comes not only as the redeemer, he comes as the subduer of Antichrist. Only that historian will have the gift of fanning the spark of hope in the past who is firmly convinced that even the dead will not be safe from the enemy if he wins. And this enemy has not ceased to be victorious. (Benjamin, 255)

Benjamin places the burden of scripture upon the capitalist machine, warning that without the subjugation of the Antichrist, even the dead will not be safe.

In Amabelle's world, the dead reside safely in perfect communion with the living. She keeps them safe by not crossing the border and returning to the nation that expelled the darker people in the year of massacres. There are only two living beings with whom Amabelle forges a deep link, Yves's mother, Man Rapadou, and Sebastien and Mimi's mother, Man Denise. Both know death well; melancholia, the antidote to Benjamin's Antichrist, compels Amabelle toward them. Man Rapadou accepts her as a daughter, without demanding that she love her lonely son in return. Man Rapadou confides to Amabelle that she realized her husband was a traitor and poisoned him, something she tells not even Yves, who imagines that his father died fighting the Yankees. She instructs Amabelle that death should come gently, like a man's hand approaching a woman's body, and confesses that she wished it would come sooner: "I wish the sun had set on my days when I was still a young, happy woman whose man was by her side, with joy in his eyes and honor in his heart" (371).

Though Amabelle never finds the same open-hearted camaraderie with Man Denise, she joins the crowd of soothsayers and venders who provide company for the grieving woman. Amabelle, long a resident of both countries, Haiti and the Dominican Republic, the dead and the living, understands Man Deinse's wish that her children would return to her from the country of the dead. Man Denise relates that her children were lined up and shot in the backs of their heads. She tells Amabelle that it is wrong for children to die far from the bones of their families, bad timing for them to go before they understand the meaning of death. Before asking Amabelle to leave so that she can be alone and "dream up my children" (324), Man Denise gives Amabelle a sense of collective anguish. She provides a shadowy map of a people tied together by melancholia.

> The tradition of the oppressed teaches us that the "state of emergency" in which we live is not the exception but the rule. We must attain to a conception of history that is in keeping with this insight. Then we shall clearly realize that it is our task to bring about a real state of emergency, and this will improve our position in the struggle against Fascism. One reason why Fascism has a chance is that in the name of progress its opponents treat it as a historical norm. The current amazement that the things we are experiencing are "still" possible in the twentieth century is not philosophical. This amazement is not the beginning of knowledge—unless it is the knowledge that the view of history which gives rise to it is untenable. (Benjamin, 257)

Taking a concrete step in her oscillation between the two worlds, Amabelle returns to River Massacre on the anniversary of the Kout Kouto, strips off her clothes, and lies on the calm waves to be reunited with the ghosts who people her life. She journeys to the site of Man Rapadou's falling, of Man Denise's dream about her children, of the sugar woman, of her mother's smile made of glass, to the place where her lover stands in a half-lit glow under the waterfall.

Amabelle's reencounter with Valencia underscores the fragility of her connection to the living, and the way that certain Dominicans passively absorbed the policy of erasure implemented by the state authorities: "All the time I had known her, we had always been dangling between being strangers and being friends. Now we were neither strangers nor friends. We were like two strangers passing each other on the street, exchanging a lengthy meaningless greeting. And at last I wanted it to

end" (401). For Valencia, it was enough to hear that Amabelle had
been killed. She did not need to seek an explanation for her death.

> To justify the 1937 massacre, Trujillo's ideologues created the myth of
> peace and national security. Accordingly, only Trujillo's use of extreme
> measures saved the Dominican Republic from "the Haitian danger."
> If the border was still intact, it was only thanks to Trujillo. Furthermore,
> official references to the 1937 massacre were absent. No documentation
> with direct references to the massacre—before, during, or after it—has
> been found in Dominican archives. It was as if it never happened. And
> for many Dominicans, misinformed by Trujillo's propaganda machine,
> it never did. (Sagás, 47)

Having witnessed the perfect mirror of the stream—a collection of
water memories, the puddle of sweat, the rising river—Amabelle bids
farewell to Valencia and returns home to sleep deeply, not interested
in recording the land of the living.

> Yet void as these tombs are of identifiable mortal remains of immortal
> souls, they are nonetheless saturated with ghostly national imagin-
> ings . . . if the nationalist imagining is so concerned, this suggests a
> strong affinity with religious imaginings. As this affinity is by no
> means fortuitous, it may be useful to begin a consideration of the cul-
> tural roots of nationalism with death, as the last of a whole gamut of
> fatalities. (Anderson, 9–10)

Benedict Anderson's evocation of ghostly national imaginings and
Freud's "death instinct" are interpellated in Amabelle. Like Haiti, symbolized by the madman searching for dawn behind the dark veil of history, Amabelle lies on the water looking for the speck of light that will
unite her with those she loves. The imagined community, or Zamora's
"usable past," leading to "the historicity of all narrative" (Zamora, 39),
emerges in the politically charged gesture of this Haitian massacre survivor, in the history pooling around Amabelle's slowly dissolving body
as she "(paddles) like a newborn in a washbasin" (414).

Benjamin tells us that massacres and tragedies are the condition of
history. Our religious and historical imagination remains rooted in
them. We must suture our knowledge of these losses with a collective
melancholia that keeps both the survivors and the dead alive. Said's
reminder of the traveling incarnations of theory speaks to those
excluded from national and global citizenship. Without public access to
privilege, caught in diasporic conditions old and new, these beings have
the messianic power to make the dead come to life. In their community

with the dead lies the ultimate power to undercut the authority of the state, to invoke powers both ancient and more formidable than the nation-states that define their existence according to a transitory ideology of white against black. Amabelle Désir, a vessel of memory and desire, contains within her the power to transmute the rules of the nation and the universe to fashion her losses to her liking. She must not be labeled as powerless or as an instrument of her master. Amabelle's trespass symbolizes her ability to exist, to exercise political right, spiritual power, to mourn beyond redemption. Overwhelming the oppressor, it is the sign of her humanity in the face of loss.

## Works Cited

Anderson, Benedict. *Imagined Communities: Reflections on the Origin and Spread of Nationalism.* London: Verso, 1983.

Benjamin, Walter. *Illuminations.* Ed. Hannah Arendt. Trans. Harry Zohn. New York: Schocken Books, 1969.

Charters, Mallay. "Edwidge Danticat: A Bitter Legacy Revisited." *Publisher's Weekly*, 245.33 (August 1998): 42–43.

Cohn, Deborah N. *History and Memory in the Two Souths: Recent Southern and Spanish American Fiction.* Nashville: Vanderbilt University Press, 1999.

Danticat, Edwidge. *The Farming of Bones* (special large print edition). Maine: Thorndike Press, 1998.

Danticat, Edwidge. "We are Ugly, but We are Here." *The Caribbean Writer*, 10 (1996). http://www.webster.edu/~corbetre/haiti/literature/danticatugly.htm

Derrida, Jacques. *Dissemination.* Trans. Barbara Johnson. Chicago: The University of Chicago Press, 1981.

Diederich, Bernard. *Trujillo: The Death of the Dictator.* Princeton: Markus Wiener Publishers, 1978.

Fanon, Frantz. *The Wretched of the Earth.* Trans. Constance Farrington. New York: Grove Press, 1968.

Freud, Sigmund. "Mourning and Melancholia." In *The Complete Psychological Works of Sigmund Freud, XIV.* London: Hogarth, 1957.

Glissant, Edouard. *Caribbean Discourse: Selected Essays.* Trans. J. Michael Dash. Charlottesville: University Press of Virginia, 1981.

Handley, George B. *Postslavery Literatures in the Americas: Family Portraits in Black and White.* Charlottesville: University Press of Virginia, 2000.

Sagás, Ernesto. *Race and Politics in the Dominican Republic.* Boca Raton: University Press of Florida, 2000.

Said, Edward. "Traveling Theory." In *The World, the Text, and the Critic.* Cambridge: Harvard University Press, 1983.

Zamora, Lois Parkinson. *The Usable Past: The Imagination of History in Recent Fiction of the Americas.* Cambridge: Cambridge University Press, 1997.